On Parade

Program Authors
Richard L. Allington
Camille L. Z. Blachowicz
Ronald L. Cramer
Patricia M. Cunningham
G. Yvonne Pérez
Constance Frazier Robinson
Sam Leaton Sebesta
Richard G. Smith
Robert J. Tierney

Instructional Consultant
John C. Manning

Program Consultants
Jesús Cortez
Alfredo Schifini
Robert E. Slavin

Critic Readers
Martha Ann Dulin
Adriana Goodier
Dorothy Kern
Betty Liddicoat
Georgina G. Lowenberg
Bob Mudrovic

**Scott, Foresman
and Company**

Editorial Office:
Glenview, Illinois

Regional Offices:
Sunnyvale, California
Tucker, Georgia
Glenview, Illinois
Oakland, New Jersey
Carrollton, Texas

Scott, Foresman Reading: An American Tradition

Gold Medal Printing

Acknowledgments

Text
Page 9: Adaptation of *Commander Toad in Space* by Jane Yolen, text copyright © 1980 by Jane Yolen, reprinted by permission of Coward, McCann & Geoghegan and Curtis Brown, Ltd.
Page 29: From *The Legend of the Bluebonnet* by Tomie dePaola, text and illustrations copyright ©1983 by Tomie dePaola, reprinted by permission of G. P. Putnam's Sons and Florence Alexander Agency.
Page 54: Text of "Nest" from *Birds* by Arnold Adoff (J. B. Lippincott). Text copyright © 1982 by Arnold Adoff. Reprinted by permission of Harper & Row, Publishers. Inc.
Page 91: From *Ty's One-man Band* by Mildred Pitts Walter, illustrations by Margot Tomes. Text copyright © 1980 by Mildred Pitts Walter, illustrations copyright © 1980 by Margot Tomes. Adapted by permission of Scholastic Inc.
Page 106: "Dinga, Dinga, Doodle" from *Treasury of Folk Songs* by Tom Glazer. Reprinted by permission of The Julian Bach Literary Agency. Copyright © 1964 by Tom Glazer.
Page 109: Reprinted by permission of Pantheon Books, a division of Random House, Inc., from *Geraldine, the Music Mouse* by Leo Lionni. Copyright © 1979 by Leo Lionni.
Page 131: Adaptation of text of *I Have a Sister, My Sister Is Deaf* by Jeanne Whitehouse Peterson. Copyright © 1977 by Jeanne Whitehouse Peterson. Reprinted by permission of Harper & Row, Publishers, Inc.
Page 140: "Robert, Who Is Often a Stranger to Himself" from *Bronzeville Boys and Girls* by Gwendolyn Brooks. Copyright © 1956 by Gwendolyn Brooks Blakely. Reprinted by permission of Harper & Row, Publishers, Inc.
Page 143: Complet text, abridged and adapted, from *Eleanor Roosevelt* by Jane Goodsell (Thomas Y. Crowell). Copyright © 1970 by Jane Goodsell. Reprinted by permission of Harper & Row, Publishers, Inc. and Marie Rodell-Frances Collin Literary Agency.
Page 160: *The Emperor's New Clothes* by Hans Christian Andersen, retold by Virginia Lee Burton. Copyright 1949 by Virginia Lee Demetrios. Copyright © renewed 1977 by George Demetrios. Reprinted by permission of Houghton Mifflin Company.
Page 183: Adapted from *Fleet-footed Florence* by Marilyn Sachs. Copyright © 1981 by Marilyn Sachs. Used by permission of Doubleday & Company, Inc.

Acknowledgments continued on page 372

ISBN 0-673-74408-6

Copyright © 1989, 1987,
Scott, Foresman and Company, Glenview, Illinois.
All Rights Reserved. Printed in the United States of America.

12345678910-RRW-979695949392919089 88

Contents

 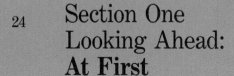

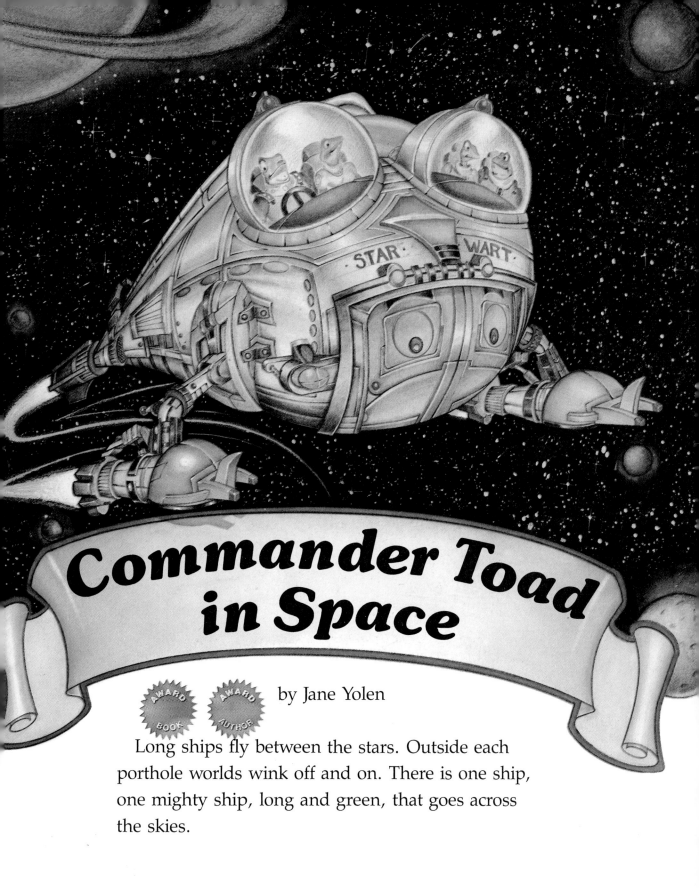

Commander Toad in Space

by Jane Yolen

Long ships fly between the stars. Outside each
porthole worlds wink off and on. There is one ship,
one mighty ship, long and green, that goes across
the skies.

The captain of this ship is brave and bright, bright and brave. There is no one quite like him in all the fleet. His name is COMMANDER TOAD. His ship is the *Star Warts*. Its mission: to go where no spaceship has gone before. To find planets. To explore galaxies. To bring a little bit of Earth out to the alien stars.

Commander Toad has a very fine crew. The copilot is Mr. Hop, who thinks deep thoughts behind his green face. Lieutenant Lily fixes engines. She loves the big machines. And young Jake Skyjumper reads the maps and plots the way from star to star. But the leader of them all is COMMANDER TOAD, brave and bright, bright and brave.

What is it that now shines on the screen with a strange and shimmering light? A brand-new world. Commander Toad speaks: "We will land and look around this brand-new world. Jake Skyjumper, you will stay on board. You others, come with me."

They get into their special suits and buckle on their special guns. "Just in case," says Commander Toad. Lieutenant Lily smiles. She is the best shot in the whole crew.

They step on board the little sky skimmer that will take them from the mother ship down to the planet below. "Wait!" It is young Jake jumping toward them.

"I have just checked this planet with our computer. The computer tells me the planet is made up of water. There is no place to land."

Mr. Hop shakes his head, puts his hand against his cheek, closes his eyes and begins to think. Lieutenant Lily stops smiling. But Commander Toad knows what to do. He runs to the ship's storeroom and takes out something big and soft and green and puts it on the floor. "What is *that?*" asks Jake Skyjumper.

"A rubber lily pad," says Commander Toad.

Lieutenant Lily smiles. "Just the thing," she says. Mr. Hop opens his eyes. They load the lily pad and a hand pump into the skimmer. And last of all comes COMMANDER TOAD.

The sky skimmer leaves the mother ship. It floats down light as milkweed fluff, noiseless as a feather in the wind. It hovers over the watery world.

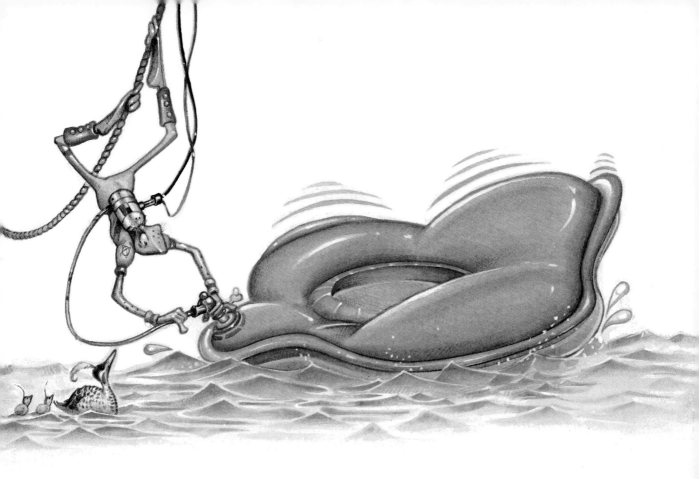

"Lieutenant," calls out Commander Toad, "drop our landing pad. You'll be a Lily with a lily. Ha ha!" He laughs at his own joke.

Lieutenant Lily opens the door. She shoves out the pad. It drifts down, lazily down, silently down, and with a little *plop* settles on the water.

Mr. Hop lets down a rope. Then Lieutenant Lily, the lightest of them all, goes down the rope. The pump is strapped to her back. She reaches the end, flips over, and holds the rope between her legs. She takes the pump from her back and starts to fill up the lily pad. Pump and pump and pump, and the lily pad is plump as a pillow.

Lieutenant Lily jumps onto it and bounces up and down to test the pad. It bobs in the water and makes little waves. But it does not sink.

Commander Toad sets the sky skimmer down until it fits right into the air-filled pad. Out comes Mr. Hop. He looks around. And last of all comes COMMANDER TOAD, brave and bright, bright and brave.

Mr. Hop closes his eyes and thinks cool thoughts behind his green face. Lieutenant Lily, taking a rest, puts her feet over the side of the pad. But Commander Toad has no time for such fiddle-faddle and folderol. He puts a hand to his ear and listens. Then Mr. Hop and Lieutenant Lily listen too.

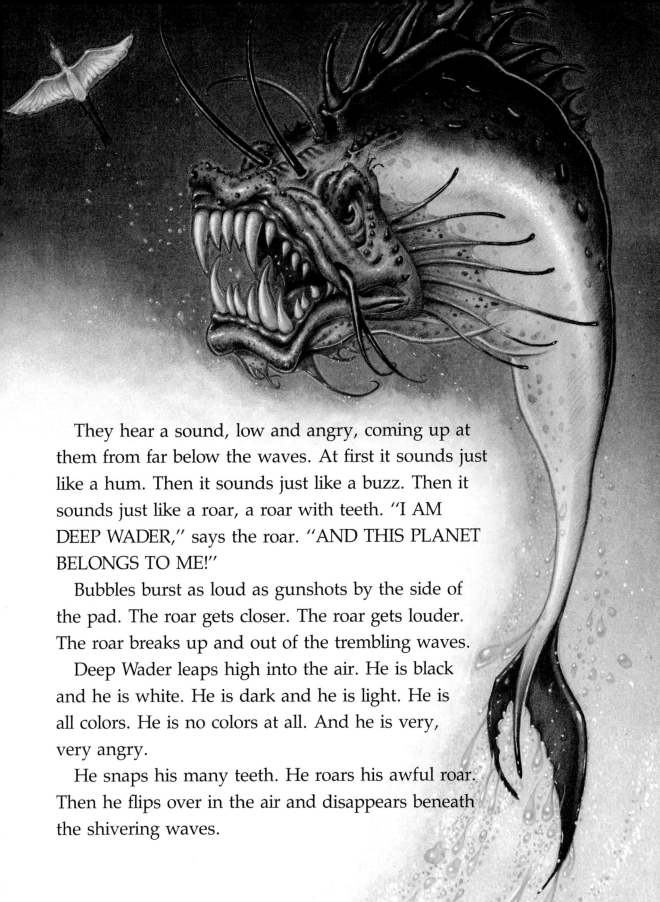

They hear a sound, low and angry, coming up at them from far below the waves. At first it sounds just like a hum. Then it sounds just like a buzz. Then it sounds just like a roar, a roar with teeth. "I AM DEEP WADER," says the roar. "AND THIS PLANET BELONGS TO ME!"

Bubbles burst as loud as gunshots by the side of the pad. The roar gets closer. The roar gets louder. The roar breaks up and out of the trembling waves.

Deep Wader leaps high into the air. He is black and he is white. He is dark and he is light. He is all colors. He is no colors at all. And he is very, very angry.

He snaps his many teeth. He roars his awful roar. Then he flips over in the air and disappears beneath the shivering waves.

And now it is silent. Too silent. The silence is fear. Into the silent fear that Deep Wader left behind, Mr. Hop speaks. "I do not think he will be gone for long," says Mr. Hop.

The other two pay attention, for Mr. Hop is seldom wrong when he has thought long and hard about something. They listen and through the silence again they hear the low and angry hum—buzz—roar coming up toward them. Lieutenant Lily kneels and aims her gun at the place where the roar will appear.

First the bubbles, then the roar break through the waves. Then the monster breaks through the waves. Deep Wader leaps up and booms through his teeth: "Mine. MINE. *MINE!*"

Lieutenant Lily shoots. She hits Deep Wader on his black skin, on his white skin, on his no-color-at-all skin. But Deep Wader only laughs as if the rays tickle him. And his laughter is more horrible than his roar. He lands with a splash and makes huge waves. The lily pad is tossed into the air and almost tips over. Lieutenant Lily and Mr. Hop and Commander Toad all hold on. But the sky skimmer slips off the pad and falls into the water. Slowly it sinks beneath the waves.

"Oh, no!" cries Lieutenant Lily. "Now how will we ever leave?"

Mr. Hop tries to think. He closes his eyes. Deep Wader swims lazily on his back toward the pad, which is bobbing like a ripe apple in a pond. He snaps his teeth and each snap makes another wave.

"My gun does not work on this monster," says Lieutenant Lily. "What should we do? Think, Hop, think!" But Mr. Hop is all thought out, and now the waves are making him seasick.

Deep Wader gets closer. His roar gets closer. His teeth get closer. His breath gets closer, too. The lily pad rocks and rolls. Commander Toad, brave and bright, bright and brave, stands up at last. He spreads his legs far apart to keep himself from falling. He takes a match from his pocket.

"This might do the trick," says Commander Toad.

Mr. Hop opens his eyes. He sighs.

"Oh, Commander," says Lieutenant Lily, "if my gun and Hop's head do not work, how can something as small as a match help?"

"You keep Deep Wader busy," Commander Toad says, "and leave the rest to me."

He takes out a small candle and lights it with the match. "I always carry candles," says Commander Toad, "in case of birthdays and other emergencies." He pulls the plug on the lily pad. Air whooshes out, then slows to a gentle breeze.

Commander Toad holds the candle up to the air hole. The flame flutters but does not go out. "Special candles," says Commander Toad. "You can blow and biow and blow some more but they never go out." Soon hot air begins to fill up the lily pad.

Mr. Hop understands, even before Lieutenant Lily. "I will keep Deep Wader busy," says Mr. Hop. "I have never yet met a monster who does not like riddles." He turns and waves his hands. He catches Deep Wader's eye. "Mr. Wader," he calls, "I have a monster riddle just for you."

Deep Wader has never had his very own riddle before. He has never had anyone to ask them. He closes his mouth and listens.

"What is a monster's favorite ballet?" asks Mr. Hop.

Deep Wader opens his mouth again. "SWAMP LAKE!" he roars. He swims closer. He no longer likes riddles.

"Keep him busy," calls Commander Toad. He lights another candle and more hot air goes into the pad.

Lieutenant Lily was once on the stage in a musical play called *Warts and Peace*. She starts to sing. Deep Wader starts to sing with her. His singing is much worse than his roar.

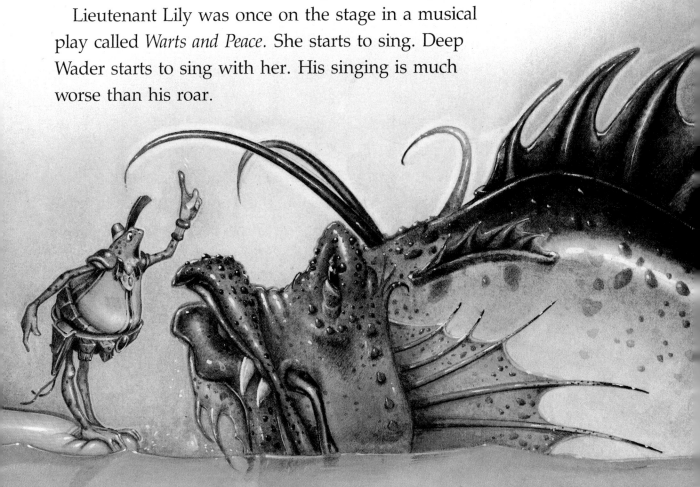

Commander Toad lights a third candle. The rubber lily pad gets bigger and bigger and bigger. It is a hot-air balloon. It begins to float one inch, then two inches, then a foot above the waves.

"NO MORE RIDDLES, NO MORE SONGS," roars Deep Wader, "LUNCH, HERE I COME."

"And here we go!" calls out Commander Toad. He puts his feet over the side and paddles quickly in the air. Lieutenant Lily and Mr. Hop do just the same.

The lily pad floats faster and faster up into the air. Deep Wader watches his lunch float away. He leaps up and snaps his teeth, but he is too late.

Commander Toad looks over the side of the lily pad. "We came in peace," he calls into Deep Wader's mouth.

"I'd like you better in pieces," Deep Wader says. "Nice *chewy* pieces." He snaps his teeth again, but the pad is out of reach.

"Just keep paddling," call Lieutenant Lily and Mr. Hop. Kick and kick and kick some more, and the lily pad rises. The three space explorers look at one another.

"That was close," says Mr. Hop. Commander Toad agrees.

"But what about being brave?" asks Lieutenant Lily.

"Bright and brave. All we did was run away."

"You cannot be brave in someone's stomach," says Mr. Hop.

"You cannot be brave unless you are first very much afraid," says Commander Toad.

"Well, I was certainly afraid," says Lieutenant Lily.

"And very, very brave," says Commander Toad.

"Keep kicking," says Mr. Hop. And they kick the lily pad all the way up to the mother ship. Young Jake Skyjumper helps them aboard.

Then the ship takes off. Brave and bright, bright and brave, Commander Toad and his crew swing *Star Warts* into deep hopper space. "Let's find some new planets," says Commander Toad.

"Where we won't have to be so brave," says Mr. Hop. They all laugh. Then they leapfrog across the galaxy from star to star to star.

1

At First

These are the first flowers of spring, a sign that a new season is beginning. The air is cold and snow lies on the ground, but the flowers have pushed through the earth to face the sun.

There are first times in people's lives too. Think about a first in your life—perhaps the first time you rode a bike or wrote your name. This Section is about firsts—how some flowers may have come to grow in Texas, the first years of a chimpanzee's life, and learning to love a new baby.

Understanding What Happens and Why

Have you ever planted radish seeds in a garden? Did radish plants grow from the seeds? Seeds need warmth, sunlight, and water to grow. If your seeds got the things they needed, plants began to grow. Just as there are reasons that things happen in a garden, there are reasons things happen in a story. Figuring out what happens and why it happens can help you understand what you read.

Words like *so* and *because* are clue words. They can help you understand what happens and why it happens. Sometimes there are no clue words. When there are no clue words in a story, the questions "What happened?" and "Why did it happen?" can help you.

As you read the paragraph about Dan's new job, ask yourself "What happened?" and "Why did it happen?"

Because Dan's alarm clock did not ring, he slept too long. It was the first day of his new job. He'd have to hurry to deliver fifty newspapers before school. He rushed into the bathroom to brush his teeth. Because he was half-asleep, in a hurry, and the tubes looked alike, Dan grabbed the wrong tube. He began to brush his teeth with face cream.

Now answer the questions.

1. What happened first?

To answer the question, look back at the first sentence. It says Dan slept too long.

2. Why did it happen?

To answer question 2, look back again at the first sentence. The word *because* is a clue word that tells why.

3. What happened to Dan when he rushed into the bathroom to brush his teeth?

4. Why did this happen?

Practicing the Skill

Read the paragraph below about why people began to wear clothes.

Long ago, people killed animals for food. They found they could use the skins of the animals for clothing. People wanted to wear clothing to protect themselves from the weather and to show other people something about themselves. Today, though clothing styles have changed, our reasons for wearing clothes are still the same.

1. Why did people kill animals?
2. What happened after they used animals for food?
3. Why did it happen?

Tips for Reading on Your Own
- Look for clue words like *so* and *because.*
- If there are no clue words, ask yourself "What happened?" and "Why did it happen?"

*In this story, a Comanche girl's sacrifice brings
something new and wonderful to the land. As you read
about the girl, you will find out what that sacrifice is and
what happens because of it.*

THE LEGEND OF THE BLUEBONNET

An Old Tale of Texas
by Tomie dePaola

"Great Spirits, the land is dying. Your People are
dying, too," the long line of dancers sang. "Tell us
what we have done to anger you. End this drought.
Save your People. Tell us what we must do so you
will send the rain that will bring back life."

For three days, the dancers danced to the sound of
the drums. For three days, the people called
Comanche watched and waited. And even though
the hard winter was over, no healing rains came.

Drought and famine are hardest on the very young
and the very old.

Among the few children left was a small girl named She-Who-Is-Alone. She sat by herself watching the dancers. In her lap was a doll made from buckskin—a warrior doll. The eyes, nose, and mouth were painted on with the juice of berries. It had beaded leggings and a belt of polished bone. On its head were brilliant blue feathers from the bird who cries "Jay-jay-jay." She loved her doll very much.

"Soon," She-Who-Is-Alone said to her doll, "the shaman will go off alone to the top of the hill to listen for the words of the Great Spirits. Then, we will know what to do so that once more the rains will come and the Earth will be green and alive. The buffalo will be plentiful and the People will be rich again."

As she talked, she thought of the mother who made the doll, of the father who brought the blue feathers. She thought of the grandfather and grandmother she had never known. They were all like shadows. It seemed long ago that they had died from the famine. The People had named her and cared for her. The warrior doll was the only thing she had left from those distant days.

"The sun is setting," the runner called as he ran
through the camp. "The shaman is returning." The
People gathered in a circle and the shaman spoke.
 "I have heard the words of the Great Spirits," he
said. "The People have become selfish. For years,
they have taken from the Earth without giving
anything back. The Great Spirits say the People must
sacrifice. We must make a burnt offering of the most
valued possession among us. The ashes of this
offering shall then be scattered to the four points of

the Earth, the Home of the Winds. When this sacrifice is made, drought and famine will cease. Life will be restored to the Earth and the People!"

The People sang a song of thanks to the Great Spirits for telling them what they must do. "I'm sure it is not my new bow that the Great Spirits want," a warrior said.

"Or my special blanket," a woman added, as everyone went to their tipis to talk and think over what the Great Spirits had asked.

Everyone, that is, except She-Who-Is-Alone. She
held her doll tightly to her heart. "You," she said,
looking at the doll. "You are my most valued
possession. It is you the Great Spirits want." And she
knew what she must do. As the council fires died out
and the tipi flaps began to close, the small girl
returned to the tipi, where she slept, to wait.

The night outside was still except for the distant
sound of the night bird with the red wings. Soon
everyone in the tipi was asleep except She-Who-
Is-Alone. Under the ashes of the tipi fire one stick
still glowed. She took it and quietly crept out into
the night.

She ran to the place on the hill where the Great Spirits had spoken to the shaman. Stars filled the sky, but there was no moon. "O Great Spirits," She-Who-Is-Alone said, "here is my warrior doll. It is the only thing I have from my family who died in this famine. It is my most valued possession I have. Please accept it."

Then, gathering twigs, she started a fire with the glowing firestick. The small girl watched as the twigs began to catch and burn.

She thought of her grandmother and grandfather, her mother and father, and all the People—their suffering, their hunger. Before she could change her mind, she thrust the doll into the fire.

She watched until the flames died down and the ashes had grown cold. Then, scooping up a handful, She-Who-Is-Alone scattered the ashes to the Home of the Winds, the North and the East, the South and the West.

And there she fell asleep until the first light of the morning sun woke her.

She looked out over the hill, and stretching out from all sides, where the ashes had fallen, the ground was covered with flowers—beautiful flowers, as blue as the feathers in the hair of the doll, as blue as the feathers of the bird who cries "Jay-jay-jay."

When the People came out of their tipis, they could scarcely believe their eyes. They gathered on the hill with She-Who-Is-Alone to look at the miraculous sight. There was no doubt about it, the flowers were a sign of forgiveness from the Great Spirits.

As the People sang and danced their thanks to the Great Spirits, a warm rain began to fall and the land began to live again. From that day on, the little girl was known by another name—"One-Who-Dearly-Loved-Her-People."

And every spring, the Great Spirits remember the sacrifice of a little girl and fill the hills and valleys of the land, now called Texas, with the beautiful blue flowers.

Even to this very day.

Meet the Author/Illustrator

Tomie dePaola never had any trouble deciding what he wanted to be when he grew up. From the time he started school, he knew he wanted to write and draw pictures for books.

DePaola loves to doodle, so he keeps pads of paper and markers everywhere. He hides his doodles in different places so they can appear later and surprise him. DePaola often gets ideas for story characters from his doodles. During a meeting at a college where he worked, Strega Nona appeared on his pad and went on to become the main character in his prize-winning book.

Tomie dePaola has written and illustrated many well-loved books for children. He has achieved his goal of creating books that he is proud of that also touch the hearts of his readers.

Comprehension Check

See your Thinker's Handbook for tips.

Think and Discuss

1. What sacrifice does She-Who-Is-Alone make?
2. What happens because of her sacrifice?
3. Why do the people call to the Great Spirits?
4. What do the Great Spirits want the people to do?
5. What two words do you think best describe She-Who-Is-Alone? Explain your choices.

• Comprehension: Cause and effect relationships

Communication Workshop

Talk

Choose a partner. Discuss whether you think She-Who-Is-Alone should have made the sacrifice that she made. What does she think about before making her sacrifice? What might have happened if She-Who-Is-Alone did not make the sacrifice? Share the reasons for your opinions with your partner.

Speaking/Listening: Cooperative learning

Write

Pretend you are She-Who-Is-Alone. Write a paragraph in your journal about the sacrifice you made, what happened because of it, and how you feel about it. Show your paragraph to your partner and ask for feedback. Does he or she think your paragraph captures the feelings you talked about?

Writing Fluency: Paragraph

At the start of her life, a baby chimpanzee has a problem. Find out what the problem is and how it changes her life. Use the graph to learn some of the information in the article in a different way.

CHIMBUKO

CONTENT-AREA
READING

by Jay Fahn

The keepers in the Great Ape House at Lincoln Park Zoo in Chicago were worried. Something was wrong with a tiny chimpanzee born on May 30, 1982, just six weeks before. The baby was weak. She was having trouble holding onto her mother. The keepers knew that a baby chimp is carried on its mother's chest and back. It must hold on tightly to eat and stay warm and safe. What could they do to help the new baby?

The zoo's director, Dr. Lester Fisher, spoke with the keepers and the veterinarian. They decided to take the baby away from her mother to try to find out what was wrong. They gave the mother some medicine that made her fall into a deep sleep. Then they took away the baby for a check-up.

A pediatrician looked at the baby chimpanzee carefully. The pediatrician found that the chimp didn't weigh as much as she should. The baby weighed scarcely three and one-half pounds, while a healthy two-month-old chimp weighs about five pounds.

The baby chimpanzee went back to live with her mother. But the baby did not get stronger. Dr. Fisher had to decide what to do. He knew that the baby chimp, like all little babies, should live with her mother. But if something weren't done, the baby might get weaker. She might even die. Dr. Fisher decided the baby would have to be raised by people for a while if she were to have a chance to become strong and healthy. People could care for her day and night. They could give her the special food and medicine she might need.

The baby chimp was moved to the nursery in the Children's Zoo on August 13. There she met Pat Sass, the keeper who would be in charge of raising her. Though other zoo workers would help, Pat would be the chimpanzee's human mother.

Pat picked an African name, Chimbuko, for the baby, since wild chimpanzees live in Africa. Before long, Chimbuko was called Chimmy.

On her first day in the zoo nursery, Chimmy made sad noises. All she wanted to do was sleep, eat, and be held closely. Pat had raised chimpanzees before, so she knew how to take care of Chimmy. A diaper kept Chimmy clean. She wore a shirt during the day and pajamas at night to keep her warm. Chimmy slept in an incubator, a heated box with glass sides. The workers watched Chimmy as she slept to make sure she was all right.

The zoo workers fed Chimmy from a baby bottle. She drank milk mixed with extra vitamins every three hours, day and night. The workers found that Chimmy drank more milk if she was being moved as she was fed. So they held Chimmy in one arm and walked as they fed her. They knew the baby needed every ounce of milk she would drink to get stronger and grow.

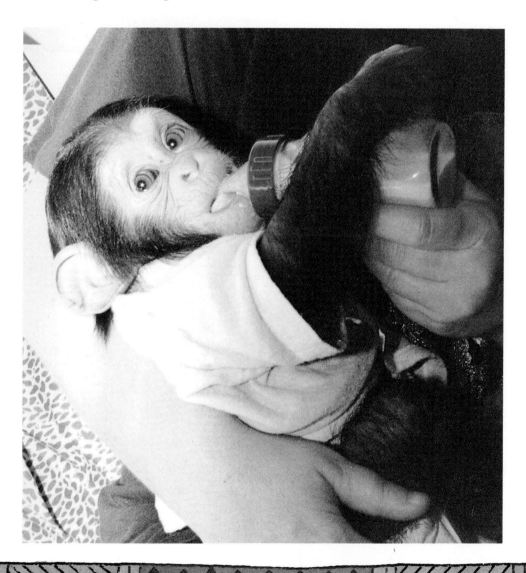

Soon Chimmy was old enough to begin eating baby cereal. The first time Pat tried to feed cereal to her, Chimmy pushed the bowl away. The spoon hit Pat. Cereal covered Pat's shirt. But it wasn't long before Chimmy liked to eat cereal. Once she began eating solid food, she began gaining weight quickly.

When Pat spent some time at home, away from her job at the zoo, Dr. Fisher let Chimmy go with her. They put a big sign on Chimmy's cage which said "Gone Fishing, Be Back Soon," so that the children who came to see Chimmy would know she was away visiting.

Chimmy stayed at Pat's house for two weeks. During that time Chimmy's baby teeth started coming in—first her upper teeth, then her lower ones. Chimmy discovered that she had fingers and toes while she was at Pat's house too. She began to wiggle her fingers and toes and play with them.

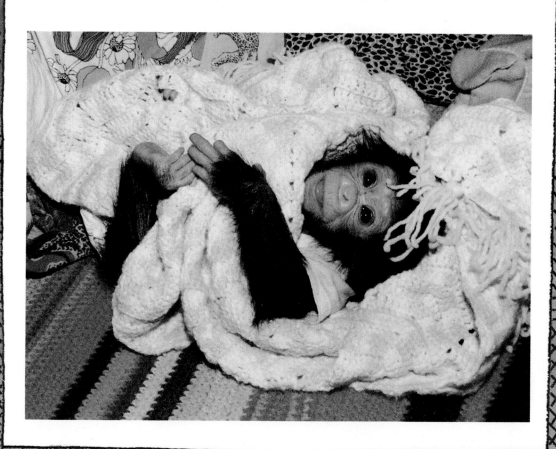

When Chimmy returned to the zoo on September 23, she weighed seven pounds, which was normal weight for her age. The workers at the zoo were no longer worried about Chimmy's health. Now they wanted to make sure Chimmy would grow and learn like the chimpanzees who live with their families do.

During her visit with Pat, Chimmy had gotten stronger. Now she began to crawl and climb. She played on a jungle gym in the nursery. But she was afraid to climb very high or swing too hard.

In the wild, chimpanzees live in large groups. To grow up properly, Chimmy needed to be with other animals. So, during the year the zoo workers introduced Chimmy to many animal friends. Chimmy was very curious about other animals. She wanted to play with them. Her best friend was Kelsey, a black leopard cub. Chimmy liked to swing down from the jungle gym, pull Kelsey's tail, and quickly climb out of reach as Kelsey turned and leaped at her.

By her first birthday, May 30, 1983, Chimmy was a happy, healthy fifteen-pound chimpanzee. Pat decided to give a birthday party for Chimmy. She invited all the people who had helped care for the baby chimp. Pat baked a birthday cake for Chimmy. She put two candles on it—one because Chimmy was a year old and the other for good luck. Chimmy was so excited that she put both her feet and her hands into the cake. She had to have a bath at her own birthday party.

Chimmy has continued to become stronger, to grow, and to learn. She has made many new friends. One friend is Nandi, a baby chimpanzee who was brought to be raised in the nursery just as Chimmy had been. Chimmy and Nandi play together almost every day. Most afternoons they have a tea party, so visitors to the zoo can see them up close. Dr. Fisher and Pat are happy that Chimmy and Nandi are together so much, since they learn things from each other that humans cannot teach them.

Chimmy eats three times a day and has a good appetite. Her favorite foods are yogurt, bananas, apples, peanuts, grapes, and hot cereal. She has come a long way from the tiny baby who could scarcely drink a few ounces of milk at a time. On Chimmy's third birthday she weighed thirty-eight pounds.

Though Chimmy has a busy, healthy life in the Children's Zoo, all the people who love her hope that a place can be found for her to live with other zoo chimpanzees. That would be the best life of all for Chimmy.

Chimmy's Weight

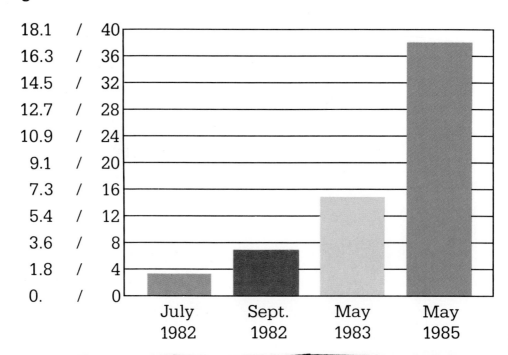

Kilograms/Pounds

		July 1982	Sept. 1982	May 1983	May 1985
18.1	/	40			
16.3	/	36			
14.5	/	32			
12.7	/	28			
10.9	/	24			
9.1	/	20			
7.3	/	16			
5.4	/	12			
3.6	/	8			
1.8	/	4			
0.	/	0			

Comprehension Check

Think and Discuss

1. What problem does Chimmy have shortly after she is born?
2. How does Chimmy's problem change her life?
3. What are some of the things that Pat does to care for Chimmy?
- 4. Does Chimmy gain more weight between July and September, 1982, or May, 1983, and May, 1985?
- 5. Use the graph to find out when Chimmy weighs seven pounds.

• Study Skill: Graphs

Communication Workshop

Talk

Interview one or two of your classmates about Chimmy. Ask them if Chimmy had a good life in the Children's Zoo, and why. Ask them why the zoo workers hope Chimmy will live with other chimps some day. Can you think of other questions to ask?

Speaking/Listening: Interviewing

Write

If you could talk to Chimmy, what questions would you ask her? Pretend you are a newspaper reporter. Write three questions you would like to ask Chimmy. Then ask a friend to answer your questions.

Writing Fluency: Questions

To be read by the teacher

Nest

by Arnold Adoff

    a bowl of grass and twigs
the
inside floor and walls of mud
                          and
bits of colored cloth
and string and tinsel woven
                     within
         grass

  a bowl of grass and twigs

  a soft place for four
            green
          blue
             eggs
under
soft sitting
    feather
      s

Use What You Know

John has just moved to a new town and wants to start borrowing books from the library. After he gets a library card, John isn't sure where to start looking for the books he wants because the library is much larger than the one he is used to.

John remembers that libraries have drawers with cards. The cards list all the books in the library. Since he knows how to use the cards in the drawers, he can find the books he wants.

Just as John used what he knew about libraries to find the books he wanted, so you can use facts you already know to understand what you read. Ask yourself:

- What is the selection about?
- What do I already know that will help me understand this selection?

When you read, use what you already know.

A new baby is a kind of beginning for a family. How does Anabel feel about her brother at first? How do her feelings change? How does the order of the events in the story show that change?

LUCKY STIFF

by Gen LeRoy

From *Lucky Stiff* by Gen LeRoy, pictures by J. Winslow Higginbottom. Text copyright © 1981 by Gen LeRoy. Illustrations copyright © 1981 by J. Winslow Higginbottom. Reprinted by permission of McGraw-Hill Book Company.

Anabel tiptoed into the nursery. She peeked at the baby again. It was still asleep. It always seemed to be sleeping, or eating, or hiccoughing, or wetting itself. Sometimes it cried . . . waah waaah waaaaH! The sound drove Anabel nuts.

Since the baby came home her mother and father seemed happier than ever. Anabel hated going off to school in the mornings because she was sure they were having a great, big, happy time when she wasn't around.

Anabel stormed into her room. She was angry. She had expected a girl baby but they brought her home a brother. A boy named Vaughan. Sounded like yawn. Everyone would laugh at his name.

Vaughan had only four hairs on his head. And no teeth. Every time he squeaked Mom and Dad would "ooh" and "aah." When she squeaked they told her to calm down. Hah! He was a real lucky stiff!

If she had trouble falling asleep, her mother would say, "Anabel, why don't you try reading a nice book?" They didn't rock her to sleep. They didn't sing her any lullabies.

Anabel got dressed, made her bed, fluffed up her pillows, fed her goldfish, and grabbed her coat. It was Saturday. She was going to play with her friend Nina. She peeked at the baby once more before she left. Lucky stiff! He was staring up at a mobile of colorful cloth birds. He was as cross-eyed as their pet Siamese cat. Anabel puffed in disgust.

    She went through her backyard, which connected
with Nina's backyard. Spike, another neighbor, was
there too. He was eating a cracker.

"Hi, Spike. Hi, Nina."

"Hi," they chorused.

"Look what I found," said Nina, "some blue chalk.
Let's play hopscotch on the sidewalk."

"OK," Spike answered gleefully.

"Nah," replied Anabel.

"How about some tag, then?" Spike suggested.

"Yes, tag," Nina agreed.

"Uh-uh, don't feel like tag," replied Anabel.

"How come?" Nina asked.

"I feel like playing house," Anabel said.

"House?" Spike was surprised.

"House?" Nina was stunned.

"Yes," Anabel said. "House."

"But what are we supposed to do?" Spike asked, eating another cracker. Anabel stood between them.

"You can be the father, Spike, and you can be the mother, Nina, and I'll be the new baby." Anabel turned around. "And look!" she pointed. "That wagon can be the crib or the baby carriage. Come on. It'll be fun! You'll see." Spike and Nina shrugged.

"Please," Anabel begged.

"Okay," they said.

Anabel lined the wagon with old material. Then she curled up inside it and began making sounds like Baby Vaughan. Spike began to laugh.

"This is silly," he said.

Suddenly Nina announced, "I think the baby's hungry." She crumpled a cracker into a plastic spoon, added water and made a mush.

"Kootchy-kootchy-koo," Spike said and tickled Anabel's chin. Then he helped Nina feed her.

Anabel wanted to spit it out. It tasted awful. But every time she let it dribble out Nina scraped it right back into Anabel's mouth.

"Yum-yum?" Nina asked.

"Yum-yum?" Spike parroted.

"Goo-goo," Anabel gurgled.

"Now, it's bedybys," Nina said.

Spike slid a pillow under Anabel's head. Nina covered her with an old rug, and they pulled the wagon through the backyard and onto the sidewalk. Then they disappeared.

Anabel didn't hear them next to her. She lifted her head. Spike and Nina were drawing a hopscotch ladder on the sidewalk.

"Hey!" she called. But they didn't look up. "Waah waaaah WAAAHHH! Nina and Spike came running.

"What's wrong, baby?" Spike asked.

"Don't be silly," Nina said. "Babies can't talk. She probably has to burp. Help me turn her over."

"Waah, wah, wah."

"What's wrong now?" Spike asked.

"Let her cry," Nina said kindly. "It's good for her lungs." They went back to their game.

Anabel didn't budge. Soon she heard other voices. She peeked over the rug. Three more friends had joined Spike and Nina. Anabel was getting sick and tired of lying around.

"Goo, goo, goo, goo!" she said loudly. Steven, Amy, and Jenny circled the wagon.

"Say hello to Uncle Steven," Spike said to Anabel.

"Say hello to Aunt Jenny and Aunt Amy," he added.

"Babies can't talk," Steven said.

"Baby want a cookie?" Amy asked. Anabel reached up to grab it but Spike took it away.

"Babies have no teeth," Spike said. Nina took the cookie, crumbled it in a spoon, added water from the hose, and fed it to Anabel. It tasted worse than the mushy cracker.

"Maybe the baby would like to watch us play?" Amy suggested.

"We better not put her on the ground," Jenny said.

"A dog might run over her."

"Or else she might eat a bug or something," Steven added.

"We have to leave babies alone so they can grow," Nina said. They left Anabel in the wagon and went back to their game.

"Kootchy-kootchy-koo," Spike said, tickling Anabel's chin before he left. She wanted to bite his finger.

Anabel stayed where she was. She watched her friends running and playing. She heard them laughing and talking. She waited a few minutes more. Then she got up, threw the rug to the ground, and walked back to her house. She passed her mother and father, who were washing their car near the garage.

She went into the house and tiptoed into the nursery. At first, she just stared at Baby Vaughan. Then she went closer to the crib. He was sleeping.

"Poor fellow," she said. "Poor little fellow." Baby Vaughan opened his eyes. "Hi," Anabel said softly. "Hello, Vaughan." She stared at his little face, his little ears and nose. "Don't worry, kid, once you learn how to talk and walk you can get out of here."

Baby Vaughan gurgled. "I'll help you learn," Anabel said in a whisper. "Whenever you're ready, okay?" Vaughan's tiny hand circled Anabel's finger. Anabel felt funny inside. Vaughan's hand was as small and as soft as a marshmallow.

"Vaughan's not such a bad name. It rhymes with dawn and lawn, so don't you worry when people laugh. Okay?" Vaughan gurgled. "Hey! I think you understand me," Anabel said. She smiled and stared at him longer.

"Well, Vaughan, I'd like to hang around and talk some more, but I have to go now." She bent over and kissed his four hairs. "We'll have another talk later." Anabel gently slid her finger away and went outside.

"Poor kid," she said to herself. "He must be bored silly." She was glad she was grown-up.

Her friends were on the front lawn teaming up to play ball. "Hey!" she called from her front porch. "Hey, you guys . . . Wait for me, will you?"

"Hurry," Nina called. Anabel ran down the steps, jumped over the gate, and joined her friends just as the game was beginning.

Comprehension Check

1. How does Anabel feel about Vaughan at first?
2. How do Anabel's feelings about Vaughan change?
3. Why does Anabel call Vaughan a lucky stiff?
- 4. Put these story events in their correct order.
   a. Anabel joins her friends as the ball game begins.
   b. Anabel is jealous of Vaughan.
   c. Anabel learns being a baby is not always fun.
   d. Baby Vaughan comes home from the hospital.
   e. Anabel tells Vaughan she will help him learn.
5. Think back to when you were very young. What could you do then that you're not allowed to do now? What can you do now that you couldn't then?

- Comprehension: Time sequence

Communication Workshop

Look through the pictures in the story with a partner. What can you learn about Anabel from them? Can you tell how old she is? What does she like to do?

Speaking/Listening: Discussion

Write a short paragraph describing Anabel that could appear in her school yearbook. Copy a picture of Anabel to tape beside your paragraph.

Writing Fluency: Paragraph

LOOKING BACK

Thinking and Writing About the Section

See your Thinker's Handbook for tips.

Prewriting

All the characters in this section have "first" experiences. You can write an explanatory paragraph to explain which story you liked the best to share with another class. To begin, copy and fill in the chart.

Story Titles	"First Experience"	Examples
Chimbuko	first years of life	discovered fingers and toes
Lucky Stiff		

Writing

Choose your favorite story and use the chart to write an explanatory paragraph. Tell what the first experience was and give several examples. Use your Writer's Handbook for more information on explanatory paragraphs.

Revising

Read your first draft to a partner. Does your topic sentence tell what will be explained? Did you include examples? Make changes, proofread, and then write a final copy.

Presenting

Read your paragraph to another class. Can they understand why the selection is your favorite?

2

Hear the Music

Think of a life without music. Imagine what would be missing if you never whistled a tune or listened to a record you love. What would it be like to have no music to dance to or songs to sing?

Music is a gift—one that people all over the world share. As you read, you will learn new things about music, but even more important you will learn something about the gift that music brings to people's lives. How are the lives of the characters changed because of music?

Figuring Out the Main Idea and Details

In a word or two, think of a name for this photo. You might pick *music* or *musicians*. Then think of a sentence that describes the most important thing in the photo. For this photo, your sentence might be *This is a group of people playing music together.*

The people and the instruments in the photo are details that tell more about the main idea.

To understand what a paragraph is all about, do the same thing. Think of one or two words that tell what the paragraph is about. This is the **topic.** Look for a sentence that tells the most important idea in the paragraph. This sentence tells the **main idea.** Knowing the main idea often helps you understand the paragraph. The other sentences in a paragraph give details about the main idea. **Details** are small pieces of information that tell more about the main idea.

Selections have main ideas. To find the main idea of a selection, first decide what the topic is. Then think of a sentence that tells the most important idea about the topic.

Read the paragraph to find out what a round is.

A round is a kind of short song for two or more singers. Usually the singers are divided into groups. Each group sings the song but starts at a different time. The song is repeated over and over again. A famous round that you may have sung or heard is "Row, Row, Row Your Boat."

Now answer the questions.

1. Which is the topic of the paragraph?
   a. rounds   b. singers

Rounds is the topic of the paragraph because this word tells what the paragraph is about.

2. Which sentence tells the main idea?
   a. A famous round that you may have sung or heard is "Row, Row, Row Your Boat."
   b. A round is a kind of short song for two or more singers.

Sentence *b* is the main idea because it tells the most important idea about rounds.

3. What details tell more about the main idea? Look at the details in the second, third, and fourth sentences.

Practicing Finding the Main Idea and Details

Read the paragraph to find out about the largest kind of piano made.

What is almost nine feet long, weighs one thousand pounds, and has twelve thousand parts? The answer is a concert grand piano. The concert grand is the largest piano made. Very few homes have rooms big enough for such a piano. The concert grand piano is made for musicians to use in concert halls.

1. What is the topic of this paragraph?
   a. concert halls
   b. concert grand pianos

2. Which sentence in the paragraph tells the main idea?

3. What are some details that tell more about the main idea?

Tips for Reading on Your Own

- Ask yourself what the paragraph is all about. This is the topic.
- Look for a sentence in the paragraph that gives the most important idea, or main idea, about the topic.
- Look for details that tell more about the main idea.

Stringed instruments around the world are very different, yet they all have some things in common. As you read the article, look for the details that show the differences and likenesses.

CONTENT-AREA
READING

Strings Around the World

by William Harrison

An audience in Philadelphia, Pennsylvania, is quiet. A gray-haired man crosses the stage. He sits down at a grand piano and begins to play. At that very minute in Tokyo, Japan, a young man plugs in an electric guitar. In Lima, Peru, a little girl practices her violin. A piano, an electric guitar, a violin—what do they have in common? All three are stringed instruments.

The third string from the left is vibrating.

The strings on instruments are different from the strings you use to fly a kite. Instrument strings **vibrate** or move quickly back and forth through the air to make a sound. It is easy to make silk, metal, and plastic strings vibrate. They are often used for instruments.

Plucking, Bowing, and Hammering

pick, a small, flat object made of wood, metal, or plastic.

There are three ways to make a sound come from a stringed instrument. You can **pluck** the strings with your fingers. That means you can pull the strings and quickly let them go. Or you can use a **pick.** You may have seen a musician pluck guitar strings with a plastic pick.

Another way to play a stringed instrument is to use a bow. A bow is a long, thin stick of wood with hair attached at each end. The hair is often from a horse's tail. The player holds the stick and pulls the hair across the string to make a singing sound.

A player can also get a sound from a stringed instrument by hitting the strings with a **hammer.** The kind of hammer a musician uses is much smaller and lighter than the kind used to drive nails into a wall. The end of the hammer is soft so it won't break the instrument.

A piano is a hammered instrument. When you press down on one of its keys, a hammer inside the piano strikes a string and makes a sound.

The Four String Families

If you travel around the world, you will find stringed instruments that are plucked, bowed, or hammered. No matter where you go, you will be able to tell the differences among stringed instruments by the way they sound and how they are played.

One other way of telling one group of stringed instruments from another is by how they look. For example, there are instruments that look like guitars in every country.

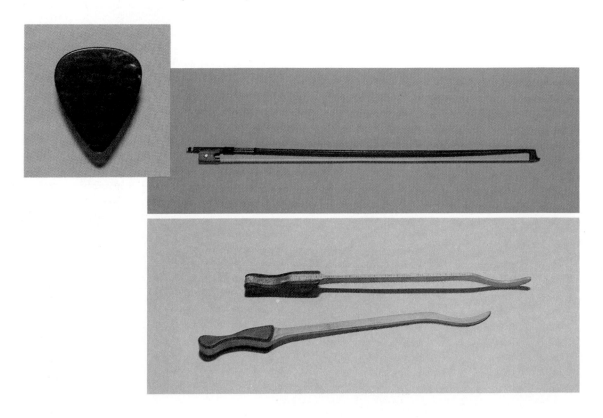

Besides their fingers, musicians use picks, bows, or hammers when they play stringed instruments.

We call instruments that look, sound, and are played alike a **family.** The stringed instrument families are the guitar family, the violin family, the zither family, and the harp family.

Let's travel around the world to find some of the many stringed instruments. During our trip you will be able to take a closer look at each of the string families.

These are instruments in the four string families.

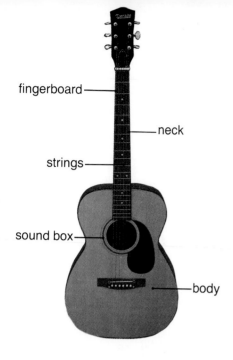

fingerboard —

neck

strings —

sound box —

body

Guitar Family

The guitar is found in many countries around the world. It is played alone as well as with other instruments.

A guitar has two main parts, a body and a neck. The strings stretch from the bottom end of the body to the top part of the neck.

The body of the guitar is one kind of **sound box.** A sound box is the part of a stringed instrument that makes the sound louder. The bigger a sound box is, the louder the sound of the instrument. Most sound boxes have a hole or holes where the sound comes out.

fingerboard, the top part of the neck where the strings touch when pressed down by the player.

The top part of the neck is the **fingerboard.** To play different notes, a musician changes the length of the strings. This is done by pressing a string down on the fingerboard with the left hand. At the same time, the right hand plucks the string.

The tar is a common guitar of Iran.

The guitars you have seen and heard have some strange-looking cousins in countries far from home. The **tar** is the most widely played guitar family instrument in Iran. Its body is made of wood and looks like two bellies stuck together. It has a long neck and metal strings. You can play twenty-six notes on each of its six strings.

Another cousin of the guitar is the **sitar.** Musicians in India have played the sitar for over seven hundred years. The sitar is a very large instrument. It has a body made of dried squash and wood. A sitar has about twenty-five metal strings. Only six or seven of them are used by the sitar player, though. The rest vibrate and give the sitar its full, ringing sound.

These African men are playing one-stringed violins.

Violin Family

There is one instrument family that can make a long singing sound. That family is the violin family. All the other stringed instruments are plucked or hammered. Plucking and hammering make short sounds. Only an instrument that can be bowed, like a violin, can make a long singing sound. This is because the string keeps singing for as long as the bow keeps moving across a string.

The violin heard most often in our country has four strings, but the simplest violins have only one string. They come from West Africa. African one-stringed violins can be found in many sizes, but they are always made the same way. The body, or sound box, is wood. A lizard-skin covering is nailed to this body. There is a hole in the skin so the sound can come out.

African violin players play alone or with singers. Their instruments sound very much like a person's voice. These violins sing along with people.

The Chinese have a violin that they rest in their laps to play. It is the **hu-chin.** The hu-chin has a tiny body and a very long neck. It has only two strings. When it is played, the neck points up to the sky.

The bow of the hu-chin passes through the strings and is attached to the instrument. The player's left hand pulls the strings to one side to make the sound higher or lower. The player also slides his or her fingers up and down the strings to make a kind of crying sound often heard in Chinese music.

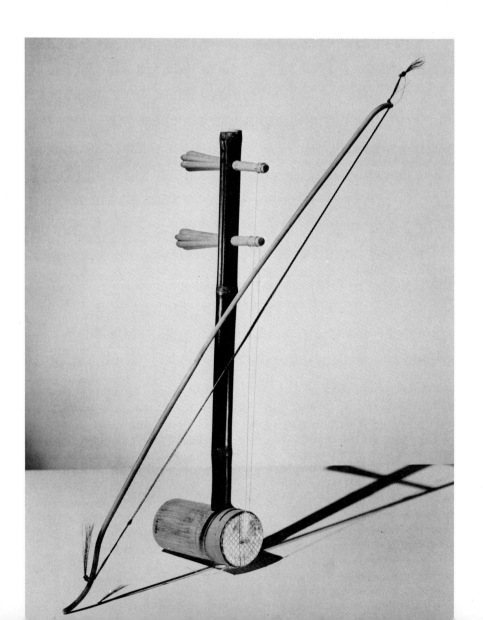

A zither can have more than forty strings.

Zither Family

A **zither** is a box with many strings stretched across the top. It has no neck as the guitar and violin do. It is plucked with fingers or a pick or struck with a **mallet.** Once you have heard the beautiful sound of a zither being struck with a soft mallet, you will never forget it.

mallet, a kind of wooden hammer with a rounded tip covered with rubber or cotton.

Musicians from Japan play a lovely zither called a **koto.** The koto's thirteen silk strings are stretched across a very large sound box. Kotos can be as long as six feet. That is why they have such a loud sound.

A koto player wears picks on three fingers of the right hand. A player gets many kinds of sounds from the instrument by plucking the strings in different places. Once in a while, the player uses the left hand to pluck. The koto has long been a favorite instrument of poets because it makes so many different sounds.

The koto is one of the largest zithers.

Another zither well-loved by poets is the santur. The **santur,** a zither from Iran, was first named in a poem written many hundreds of years ago. This poem tells a story about birds playing instruments. The birds must have played the santur with their beaks since it is a hammered instrument.

Though the santur is much smaller than the koto, it has seventy-two strings. It would be very hard to play if each string made a different note. But every set of four strings makes the same note.

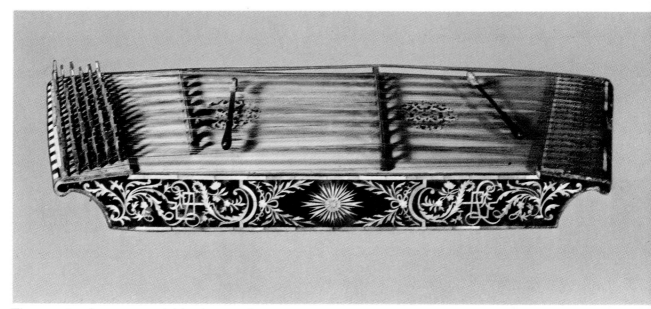

The santur is a very old instrument.

The women shown on this Greek vase are playing harps.

This harp was played by Irish musicians long ago. You can still hear the Irish harp today.

The harp most often heard in the United States has forty-six strings.

Harp Family

The harp is different from the other stringed instruments. An open frame with one or more strings stretched across it, the harp is the simplest stringed instrument. Most harps have no body, no sound box, and no neck. The harp is most often plucked with the fingers and thumbs of both hands.

Sounds of Strings

The stringed instruments of the world have many shapes and are many sizes. They are built of wood, metal, plastic, and other things. They look and sound very different from one another, but all stringed instruments are plucked, bowed, or hammered.

The next time you see a stringed instrument, try to figure out whether it belongs to the guitar family, the violin family, the zither family, or the harp family. If you have not heard the differences among the stringed instruments, perhaps one day you will.

All over the world you can hear the sounds of strings.

Comprehension Check

Think and Discuss

1. How are all the instruments in the article alike?
2. How are the instruments different?
• 3. Reread the first paragraph on page 86.
   a. What is the topic?
   b. Which sentence tells the main idea?
   c. What details tell more about the main idea?
4. Which instrument would you like to play? Why?
• 5. What is the main idea of the article?
   a. Stringed instruments make the most beautiful music.
   b. Stringed instruments around the world are different yet alike in some ways.

See your Thinker's Handbook for tips.

• Comprehension: Main idea and supporting details

Communication Workshop

Talk

Get together with a friend and discuss how you could make a stringed instrument with rubber bands, a tissue box, tape, wire, a shoebox, and a stapler.

Speaking/Listening: Discussion

Write

Write a paragraph that tells exactly how to make your stringed instrument. Share it with your friend.

Writing Fluency: Paragraph

*One hot summer night a man brings a special gift to a
town. Meet Andro, the one-man band. Learn about the gift
he brings. Why is Andro's gift special? What conclusion
can you draw about the one-man band?*

Ty's One-man Band

by Mildred Pitts Walter

The sun rose aflame. It quickly dried the dew and
baked the town. Another hot, humdrum day. Ty's
mother was washing clothes, his father was busy
unloading feed for the chickens, and his sister was in
the kitchen. Ty had nothing fun to do.

He knocked on his brother's door. "Jason," he
asked, "want to come to the pond with me?"

"I'm busy," Jason said as he combed his hair. "Besides, it's too hot to go out today."

Ty thought of the tall, cool grass at the pond and decided to go there alone.

At the pond, big trees sank their roots down deep and lifted their branches up, up, up toward the sky. The grass grew tall enough to hide a boy as big as Ty. He lay quiet, listening. Step-th-hump . . . Ty pressed his ear to the ground. He heard it again: Step-th-hump, step-th-hump, step-th-hump.

What could it be? Ty sat up, his heart beating wildly as he kept still, listening. Step-th-hump; step-th-hump. Not a slither, not a snake, not a raccoon with her babies coming to fish in the pond. Raccoons grunt when hunting food and their babies make loud churr-rr-rrr, churr-rrr-rrrs like a kitten's soft purr-rrr.

Step-th-hump; step-th-hump; step-th-hump, closer it came. Then Ty saw a man carrying a bundle. Ty had never seen anyone like this before. The man had only one leg. The other leg was nothing but a wooden peg.

The man walked down the path to the water's
edge and set his bundle down. Then he bent his one
knee, and with his peg leg balanced in the air, he
washed his face and hands in the pond. He looks
like a dancer, Ty thought.

The man took his time unfolding a red cloth. From
the bundle he took a tin cup, a tin plate, and a
spoon. Then he took out cheese, apples, and a big
round loaf of bread. He nibbled the cheese to taste it.
He smiled and then he ate hungrily.

He washed his dishes in the pond and then did a
surprising thing. He tossed his cup into the air and
caught it. He tossed the plate and then the spoon.
He's a juggler! Ty thought.

Again the man tossed the cup, plate, and spoon in the air one after the other, over and over and over very quickly and caught them all. Then he beat a rhythm with the spoon on the cup: tink-ki-tink-ki-ki-tink-ki-tink, tink-ki-tink-ki-ki-tink-ki-tink; and on the plate: tank-ka-tank-ka-ka-tank-ka-tank, tank-ka-tank-ka-ka-tank-ka-tank; and then on the cup and plate: tink-ki-tink-ki-tank, tink-ki-tink-ki-tank, tink-ki-tank-ka-tank, tink-ki-tank-ka-tank, tank-ka-tink-ka-tink-ka-tank, tank-ka-tink-ka-tink-ka-tank.

He's a drummer, too, Ty said to himself. Wonder if he's a circus man.

Ty still watched from the cool tall grass. The sun moved slowly up to the center of the sky. Nothing stirred in the heat. Then there was a low rumble like thunder afar and a train turned the bend: woo-woo-woo-ee-ee-eee. Soon there was another thunderous roar and a loud WOO-WOO-WOO-OO-EEE! Ty forgot the man and watched the train speed by, clackety-clackety-clackety-clack. The woo of the whistle and the clack of the wheels died away. Ty looked toward the pond for the man, but he was no longer there.

Ty peeped out of the tall grass. He looked to the left, then to the right and all around. How had the man disappeared so quickly, Ty wondered.

Did he see me and hide? But where could he hide
so quickly?

Slowly Ty moved out of the grass and quietly
moved toward the trail. The crackle of twigs sounded
like fireworks. He kept looking for the stranger. He
looked in the bushes near the pond. Where had the
man gone? Was he a disappearing magician, too? Ty
tiptoed to the trail. He felt his heart beat thump,
thump.

Just as he was almost to the trail—WHEE-EET!

Ty screamed and froze.

The man jumped out of the grass and laughed. He laughed so hard that Ty began to laugh, too.

"Why are you tiptoeing around like that?" the man finally asked.

"I was looking for you. I thought you had disappeared," Ty said.

"Did you think I wasn't real? I didn't mean to scare you," the man said. "I only whistled for fun."

"Do it again," Ty said.

The man did it again. Then he whistled a tune and danced a step.

"Are you a circus man?" Ty asked.

"No. I'm not a circus man."

"Who are you?"

"My name is Andro and I'm a one-man band."

"What's a one-man band?"

"I'll show you. Go home and get a washboard and two wooden spoons, a tin pail and a comb. I'll come into town at sundown and make music for you and your friends."

Ty hurried home. A one-man band! Could he remember all those things to get? Wooden spoons, a tin pail, a washboard . . . there was another thing. What had he forgotten? Ty scratched his head and tried to think. A comb!

Wait'll I tell my friends, he thought. They'll come and hear the music, too.

At home Ty ran to Jason's room.

"Can I use your comb at sundown for the one-man band?"

"For the what?" Jason asked.

Ty told Jason about the man. "Come and bring your friends at sundown!" he said.

"Don't be silly. How can he make music with just those old things? My friends will laugh and yours will too if you try to tell them such a thing."

"But can I use your comb?"

"Yea, but combs are made for combing hair, not for making music."

Ty rushed to the kitchen where his sister was stirring corn bread. He told her about the man who was a band. "Can I use two wooden spoons at sundown?"

"Yea," his sister said, "if you promise to bring them back. These spoons have made a lot of good corn bread, but I never heard them make music." She laughed as Ty rushed off.

He found his mother in the yard, taking in clothes. He told her about Andro.

She shook her head and said, "You may use my washboard at sundown. But that board is made for washing, not for making music."

His father was in the shed, putting corn in the pail to feed the chickens. "Of course, you may use the pail, son, but don't bet on hearing a one-man band. Pails are for hauling, not music."

Ty ran to tell his friends. No one believed there was such a thing as a one-man band. How could a man dance and make music with a comb, washboard, or wooden spoons? Jason was right. All of Ty's friends laughed.

The sun turned into a glowing red ball. It sank lower and lower, but the town didn't cool. People fanned themselves on their porches. Ty's friends sat in their yards or sprawled on their steps. It was so hot they didn't even talk.

Ty sat on the corner under the street lamp with the comb, the pail, two wooden spoons, and the washboard. He waited. Would Andro come? And if he came, what kind of music would he make with Jason's comb, the old washboard, two wooden spoons, and a pail?

Twilight turned purple. Had Andro forgotten? Soon the street light came on and Ty's friends saw him still waiting.

"Hey, so you think the one-man band is coming, eh?" Ivan shouted.

"If he were coming, he'd be here by now," Nohl called.

"Washboard music? What's that?" Josh said as they all laughed.

"He will come. You'll see," Ty shouted at them.

Ty waited and waited. Could Andro find his way into town? Would he come? Ty waited some more. He was just about to pick up his things and go home.

Then in the darkness he heard a step-th-hump, step-th-hump, step-th-hump. He was coming! "Whee-ee-ttt! Whee-tt! Whee-ee-ttt!" Andro whistled.

Before Ty could speak, Andro turned upside down and walked toward Ty on his hands. "I'm here at your service," he said. He turned right side up and bowed low.

Ty just grinned.

Andro looked at all the things. He turned them about one by one. "These will make fine music," he said as he sat with his good leg folded under him.

He placed the spoons between his fingers and moved them very fast. Quack-quacket-t-quack. The empty square filled with the sound of ducks. Then he made the sound of horses dancing slowly,

clip-clop-clip-clop-clop. They danced faster,
clipty-clop, clipty-clop, clipty-clop-clop. Faster still,
cl-oo-pop, cl-oo-pop, cl-oo-pop-pop-pop-pop-pop.
"Hi ho, Silver!" Andro shouted.

Ty clapped and clapped. Andro took a thin piece of
tissue paper from his pocket and carefully folded the
paper over the comb. Before Ty could ask what that
was all about, Andro was making music.

Ty sang along when Andro played. The music
drifted through the empty streets, around quiet
corners. One by one people began to leave their
porches. They pressed in closer and clapped their
hands and tapped their feet as Andro played and
danced to his own music.

His peg leg went tap-tap-ti-ti-tappity-tap,
tappity-tap-tap-ti-ti-tap. He twirled, skipped, hopped,
and danced 'round and 'round in the spotlight of the
street lamp.

Andro stopped dancing and began to make sounds on the washboard. As he passed his fingers over the board, Ty could hear water falling, rushing down a hill over rocks, then gurgling in a stream, and then trickling to a drip, like from a faucet. Best of all were sounds of a big freight train puffing slowly, then faster, faster, faster still, then passing by with the whistle far away.

"More!" Ivan shouted.

Andro sat down, held the pail under his arm, and with his fingers drummed: di-di-did-d-d-dum, did-di-d-d-dum, de-le-di-di-doo, de-le-di-di-doo, diddle-dum-dum-doo, diddle-dum-dum-doo.

"More! More!" Josh and Nohl cried.

Andro set the pail down. With a spoon in his hand, he hit the pail, his wooden leg, and the other spoon. Di-de-le-dum, di-de-le-dum, de-di-la-di-ti-do, de-di-la-de-ti-do, chuck-chick-chu-dum, chick-chick-chu-dum.

Boys and girls, mothers and fathers, even the babies clapped their hands. Some danced in the street. When the music stopped, everybody shouted, "More!"

Andro let Ty take turns using the instruments. Ty's friends wanted turns, too, and soon the four of them played together like a one-man band. Everybody danced. Only Ty saw Andro slip away back into the night.

Comprehension Check

Think and Discuss

- 1. What gift does Andro bring to the town?
- 2. Why is Andro's gift so special?
- 3. What does Andro use to make music?
- 4. Why don't Ty's friends and family believe in the one-man band at first?
- 5. How do Ty's friends and family feel about the one-man band at the end of the story?

Comprehension: Draws conclusions

Communication Workshop

Talk

Andro, the one-man band, is a sort of mystery. We learn about his music, but we do not learn much about the man himself. Get together with a friend and solve the mystery of Andro. Discuss where you think he came from. What does he do in his free time?

Speaking/Listening: Cooperative learning

Write

Write a news article about Andro for a city newspaper. Pretend you are there the night Andro plays in Ty's town. After the show, you interview him. Include quotes in your article that Andro might have said. Tell interesting things about the man. Read your article aloud to the class.

Writing Fluency: News article

Following Directions

Would you like to make a musical comb? Here are directions to help you. The directions list the steps to follow to make the musical comb.

First, read through the directions slowly and look at the picture. Make sure you understand what you are to do. Then get all the things you need. Follow the directions carefully and you will be making music in no time.

Musical Comb

You will need
- a fine-toothed comb
- a piece of waxed paper
- a pair of scissors

1. Cut the waxed paper so that it is the same length as the comb and twice as wide. Fold the paper over the comb, leaving about ⅛″ space between the fold and the comb.

2. With the teeth of the comb pointing up, hold the comb and paper at both ends.

3. Press your mouth against the side of the comb and hum a tune. Move your mouth from one end of the comb to the other to make the waxed paper vibrate against the comb.

Dinga Dinga Doodle

Did you ev-er see a cow in the sky?

She would fall if____ she did try.

2.

Did you ever see the sun at night?
I never did, Of course, you're right.
How can the sun shine at night
When day begins when it gives light?

Dinga, Dinga Doodle, dinga dinga dite,
It's always day when the sun is bright.

3.

Did you ever see a rose in the snow?
I never did. The answer is no.
How can a rose bloom in the snow
When it's too cold for it to grow?

Dinga dinga doodle, dinga dinga dow,
A rosebush sleeps when the cold
    winds blow.

4.

Did you ever see a little boy cry?
Yes, I did. And so did I.
It seems such a shame for a boy to cry
When he could laugh if he did try.

Dinga dinga doodle, dinga dinga dye,
It's better to laugh than it is to cry.

Geraldine finds something she loves as much as cheese. What do Geraldine's thoughts and actions tell you about her? Do you think it takes a very special character to make a discovery like Geraldine's?

Geraldine, the Music Mouse

by Leo Lionni

Geraldine had never heard music before. Noises, yes. Many noises—the voices of people, the slamming of doors, the barking of dogs, the rushing of water, the meows of cats in the courtyard. And, of course, the soft peeping of mice. But music, never.

Then one morning . . .

In the pantry of the empty house where Geraldine lived, she discovered an enormous piece of Parmesan cheese—the largest she had ever seen. Eagerly, she took a little bite from it. It was delicious. But how would she be able to take it to her secret hideout in the barn?

She ran to her friends who lived next door and told them about her discovery.

"If you help me carry it to my hideout," she said, "I'll give each of you a big piece."

Her friends, who loved cheese, happily agreed. "Let's go!" they said. And off they went.

"It's enormous! It's gigantic! It's immense! It's fantastic!" they shouted with joy when they saw the piece of cheese.

They pushed and pulled and tugged and finally they managed to carry it to Geraldine's hideout.

There, Geraldine climbed to the very top of the cheese. She dug her little teeth into it and pulled away crumb after crumb, chunk after chunk.

As her friends carried away their cheese tidbits, Geraldine peered in amazement at the hole she had gnawed. There she saw the shapes of two enormous ears—cheese ears!

As soon as her friends were gone, she went back to work again. She nibbled away at the cheese as fast as she could. When she was halfway through, Geraldine climbed down to have a look at the forms she had freed. She could hardly believe what she saw. The ears were those of a giant mouse, still partly hidden, of solid cheese. To its puckered lips it held a flute. Geraldine gnawed and gnawed until she had finally uncovered the entire mouse.

Then she realized that the flute was really the tip of the mouse's tail. Astonished, exhausted, and a little frightened, Geraldine stared at the cheese statue. With the dimming of the last daylight she fell asleep.

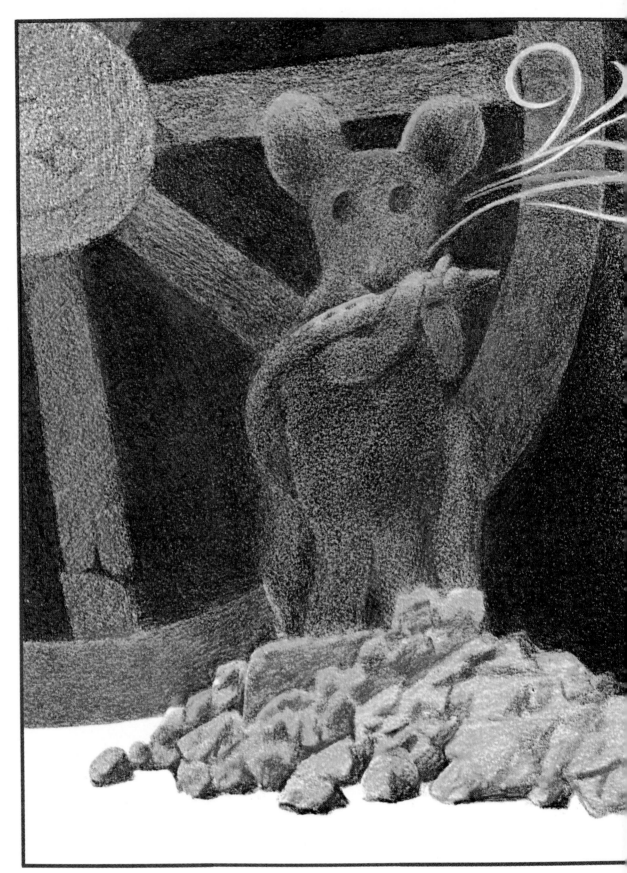

Suddenly she was awakened by some strange sounds. They seemed to come from the direction of the mouse's flute. She jumped to her feet. As it grew darker, the sounds became clearer and more melodious until they seemed to move lightly through the air like invisible strings of silver and gold. Never had Geraldine heard anything so beautiful.

"Music!" she thought. "This must be music!"

She listened all through the night until the first glow of dawn filtered through the dusty windowpanes.

But as the cheese mouse was slowly bathed in light, the music became softer, until it stopped altogether.

"Play, play," Geraldine begged. "Play some more!"

But not a sound came from the flute.

"Will it ever play again?" Geraldine thought as she gobbled up some of the crumbs that lay around.

When the next evening approached, it brought the answer to her question. The music began faintly at dusk and lasted until the break of day. And so, night after night, the cheese flutist played for Geraldine. She learned to recognize the melodies, and even in daylight they lingered in her ears.

Then one day she met her friends on the street. They were desperate.

"Geraldine!" they said. "We have no more food, and there is none to be found anywhere. You must share your cheese with us."

"But that is not possible!" Geraldine shouted.

"Why?" asked the others, angrily.

"Because . . . because . . . because it is MUSIC!"

Her friends looked at Geraldine, surprised.

"What is music?" they asked all together.

For a moment Geraldine stood deep in thought. Then she took a step backward, solemnly lifted the tip of her tail to her puckered lips, took a deep breath and blew. She blew hard. She puffed, she peeped, she tweeted. She screeched. Her friends laughed until their hungry little tummies hurt.

Then a long, soft, beautiful whistle came from Geraldine's lips. One of the melodies of the cheese flute echoed in the air. The little mice held their breath in amazement. Other mice came to hear the miracle. When the tune came to an end, Gregory, the oldest of the group, whispered, "If this is music, Geraldine, you are right. We cannot eat that cheese."

"No," said Geraldine, joyfully. "Now we CAN eat the cheese. Because . . . now the music is in me."

With that they all followed Geraldine to the barn. And while Geraldine whistled the gayest of tunes, they ate cheese to their tummies' content.

Meet the Author/Illustrator

Leo Lionni has been interested in art ever since he was a young child in Holland. He remembers drawing plants and animals when he was in grade school.

Lionni moved to the United States and soon became an artist. His first book, *Little Blue and Little Yellow*, "just happened" after he told a story about the meeting of a blue spot and a yellow spot to his grandchildren and made the story into a sample book. Lionni has been writing books for children—and adults—ever since. "I really don't make books for children at all. I make them for that part of us, of myself and of my friends, which has never changed, which is still a child," he says.

Lionni finds writing a story harder than illustrating it. He likes to illustrate his stories with different types of art—drawings, crayon pictures, and pictures made of pasted bits of paper. Many of his books, such as *Swimmy*, *Inch by Inch*, and *Alexander and the Wind-up Mouse*, have won awards.

Lionni now lives in Italy. He plays music for fun, but he says he would like to be a better musician. Clearly Geraldine shares the author's love of music.

Comprehension Check

Think and Discuss

1. What does Geraldine discover that she loves as much as cheese?
2. How do you know that music becomes very important to Geraldine?
 • 3. Which two words best describe Geraldine: *silly, musical, talented, angry?*
 • 4. Is Geraldine an artist? Why or why not?
5. In what ways is music important in your life?

 • Comprehension: Character

Communication Workshop

Talk

Now that the mice have music, what will be different in their lives? Get together with a group of your classmates and brainstorm ideas. Will the mice learn to dance? Will their children like the same music the adults do? Will they play music loudly enough to give away their hiding places?

Speaking/Listening: Group discussion

Write

Write a story to show what Geraldine and her friends do now that they have music. Share your story with your classmates during a Story Swap.

Writing Fluency: Story

LOOKING BACK

See your Thinker's Handbook for tips.

Prewriting

Thinking and Writing About the Section

In this section, you learned about music and several musical instruments. By using the pictures as well as what you read, you can write an explanatory paragraph about how to play one of the instruments to share with your class. First copy this chart and talk with a partner to fill it in.

Selection Title	Instrument: Name and How to Play
"Strings Around the World"	zither: pluck with fingers, a pick, or strike with mallet
"Ty's One-man Band"	
"Geraldine, the Music Mouse"	

Writing

Write an explanatory paragraph about how to play one of these instruments. Be sure your explanation is clear. Use your Writer's Handbook for more help.

Revising

Read your first draft to a partner. Can he or she understand your explanation? Make changes, proofread, and write a final copy.

Presenting

Draw a picture of the instrument on your final copy. Display your paper on a class bulletin board.

3

Being Yourself

As this artist is painting a picture of herself she is asking "Who am I?" and "What do I want to show people about myself?" Sometimes it is not easy to answer questions like these. It can be hard to be yourself when other people seem to want you to be like them.

Being yourself is something all the characters in this Section have to think about. How can a deaf girl be herself and also fit into a family that can hear? How can a young woman overcome shyness to stand up for her ideas? How can a king learn to trust himself?

Figuring Out the Author's Purpose

Imagine that you get a letter from your best friend, who is away at summer camp. Your friend has three reasons for writing the letter. His first reason is to tell you about camp. He wants to tell you what camp looks like and what he does there. His second reason is to entertain you by telling you a funny story about how some frogs got into the beds. His third reason is to get you to come to camp next summer.

A person writing a letter and an author of a book or story have a purpose for writing. The **purpose** is the reason or reasons the author has for writing. One reason is to **inform,** or tell the reader something. A second is to **entertain** or give enjoyment. A third is to **persuade,** or get the reader to think a certain way or do something. Looking for these reasons can help you understand what you read.

As you read the story below, ask yourself why the author may have written it. While you are reading, remember to look for the three common reasons for writing: to inform, to entertain, to persuade.

Have you ever been to summer camp? There is always so much to do there, from swimming and sailing to telling scary stories at night.

Do you like to have a good time? Do you like to make new friends? Then come to summer camp. Write to Ben Decker at Camp Hudson for more information.

Now answer the following questions.

1. Is the author mainly trying to inform, entertain, or persuade you?

The author wants you to come to camp. Did you remember that when an author tries to get you to do something, the author's purpose is to persuade?

2. What are two ideas that the author uses to persuade you?

The author tells you about the good times and meeting new friends at camp.

3. Does the author write any sentences that tell what happens at camp?

4. Is the second purpose to inform or to entertain?

Practicing Figuring Out the Author's Purpose

Read about a tramp clown. Think about the author's purpose for writing.

We put on a circus at camp this summer. My brother, Jim, was a tramp clown. A tramp clown wears dark grease paint on his face and dresses in loose, patched clothes.

When Jim shuffled into the ring in his tramp outfit, I laughed so hard I spilled popcorn on Dinah's head. Then she started laughing. Pretty soon everyone was roaring with laughter. Maybe I should be a clown too!

1. What is a tramp clown?
2. Did the author write any sentences to make you smile?
3. What are the author's two purposes?

Tips for Reading on Your Own

- Think about why the author may have written the selection.
- Was it to inform?
- Was it to entertain?
- Was it to persuade?

In this nonfiction selection, an older sister tells about her younger sister, who is deaf. She tells what it is like to live with a deaf person. Think about the reason the author may have had for writing this selection.

I Have a Sister
My Sister is Deaf

by Jeanne Whitehouse Peterson

I have a sister.
My sister is deaf.
She is special.
There are not many sisters like mine.

My sister can play the piano.
She likes to feel the deep rumbling chords.
But she will never be able to sing.
She cannot hear the tune.

My sister can dance with a partner or march in a line.
She likes to leap, to tumble, to roll,
to climb to the top of the monkey bars.
She watches me as we climb.
I watch her, too.
She cannot hear me shout "Look out!"
But she can see me swinging her way.
She laughs and swings backward, trying to catch my legs.
I have a sister who likes to go with me
out to the grassy lot behind our house.
Today we are stalking deer.
I turn to speak to her. I use no voice,
just my fingers and my lips.
She understands, and walks behind me,
stepping where I step.
I am the one who listens for small sounds.
She is the one who watches
for quick movements in the grass.

When my sister was very small,
when I went to school and she did not,
my sister learned to say some words.
Each day she sat on the floor with our mother,
playing with some toys we keep in an old shoe box.
"It's a ball," our mother would say.
"It's a dog. It's a book."
When I came home, I also sat on the floor.
My sister put her hands into the box.
She smiled and said, "Ball."
Baaaal it sounded to me.
"It's a ball," I repeated, just like our mother did.
My sister nodded and smiled.
"Ball," she said once more.
Again it sounded like *baaal* to me.

Now my sister has started going to my school,
although our mother still helps her speak, sign, and
lip-read at home.
The teacher and children do not understand every
word she says, like *sister* or *water* or *thumb*.
Today the children in her room told me,
"Your sister said *blue!*"
Well, I heard her say that a long time ago.
But they have not lived with my sister for five years
the way I have.

I understand my sister.
My sister understands what I say too,
especially if I speak slowly while I sign.
But it is not only my lips and fingers that
my sister watches.
I wore my sunglasses yesterday.
The frames are very large. The lenses are very black.
My sister made me take them off when I spoke.
What do my brown eyes say to her brown eyes?
That I would really rather play ball than play house?
That I just heard our mother call,
but I do not want to go in yet?

Yes, I have a sister who can understand what I say.
But not always.
Last night I asked, "Where are my pajamas?"
She went into the kitchen and brought out a bunch of
bananas from the fruit bowl on the table.

My friends ask me about my little sister.
They ask, "Does it hurt to be deaf?"
"No," I say, "her ears don't hurt,
but her feelings do when people do not understand."

My sister cannot always tell me with words
what she feels.
Sometimes she cannot even show me with her hands.
But when she is angry or happy or sad,
my sister can say more with her face and her shoulders
than anyone else I know.

I tell my friends I have a sister
who knows when a dog is barking near her
and who says she does not like the feel of that sound.
She knows when our cat is purring
if it is sitting on her lap,
or that our radio is playing
if she is touching it with her hand.

But my sister does not know if the telephone is ringing
or if someone is knocking at the door.
She will never hear the garbage cans
clanging around in the street.

I have a sister who sometimes cries at night,
when it is dark and there is no light in the hall.
When I try plugging my ears in the darkness,
I cannot hear the clock ticking on the shelf
or the television playing in the living room.
I do not hear any cars moving out on the street.
There is nothing.
Then I wonder, is it the same?

I have a sister who will never hear the branches
scraping against the window of our room.
She will not hear the sweet tones of the wind chimes
I have hung up there.
But when the storms come,
my sister does not wake to the sudden rolling thunder,
or to the quick *clap-clap* of the shutters in the wind.
My little sister sleeps.
I am the one who is afraid.

When my friends ask, I tell them
I have a sister who watches television
without turning on the sound.
I have a sister who rocks her dolls
without singing any tune.
I have a sister who can talk with her fingers
or in a hoarse, gentle voice.
But sometimes she yells so loud,
our mother says the neighbors will complain.

I stamp my foot to get my sister's attention,
or wave at her across the room.
I come up beside her and put my hand on her arm.
She can feel the stamping.
She can feel the touching.
She can glimpse my moving hand
from the corner of her eye.
But if I walk up behind her and call out her name,
she cannot hear me.

I have a sister.
My sister is deaf.

Comprehension Check

1. What are two ways living with the deaf sister in the selection is different from living with a sister who can hear?
2. How does the younger sister understand what people say?
3. Why is it important for the younger sister to see the eyes of someone who is talking?
4. What is the main reason the author wrote the story?
5. What games could you play with someone who is deaf?

e your Thinker's ndbook for tips.

• Comprehension: Author's purpose

Communication Workshop

Talk

Get together with a friend and list all kinds of sounds you hear during the day. Then read through your list together. Put a star beside those sounds you would miss the most if you were deaf. Put an *X* beside the sounds you would be glad not to hear.

Speaking/Listening: Cooperative learning

Write

Write a paragraph about some of the sounds you enjoy hearing every day. Try to make a recording of the sound. Play it in the background as you read your paragraph to the class.

Writing Fluency: Paragraph

Robert, Who Is Often a Stranger to Himself

by Gwendolyn Brooks

Do you ever look in the looking-glass
And see a stranger there?
A child you know and do not know,
Wearing what you wear?

Prefixes

Both these dogs have won a ribbon at the Growl Dog Show. Look at the words on the ribbons. You will see a root word you know. A word part was added to the beginning of the root word.

Sometimes root words have word parts called **prefixes** added to them. A prefix is added to the beginning of a root word to make a new word. The prefix *over-* means "above normal," "too much," or "too long." The prefix *under-* means "below," "less than normal," or "not enough."

Read the following words: *oversleep, undercook.*
What are the root words? What prefix is added to
each root word? What does each word mean?

In *oversleep,* the root word is *sleep.* The prefix is
over-. Oversleep means "sleep too long."

In *undercook,* the root word is *cook.* The prefix is
under-. Undercook means "cook not enough."

Practicing Prefixes

Read the paragraph. Name the root word and the
prefix of the underlined words. Then tell the meaning
of the words.

My dog, Chipper, is the fastest dog in the
neighborhood. Even though she is small, she races
the <u>overgrown</u> and <u>overfed</u> dogs on the block. When
she beats the big dogs in a race, I give her a bone
that she buries <u>underground</u>.

Tips for Reading on Your Own

- When you see a word with a prefix, look to see if you
know the root word.
- Use the meaning of the prefix to help you figure out
the meaning of the word.
- For more tips on figuring out words, see your Word
Study Handbook.

A shy, lonely little girl grows up to be one of the best-known and best-loved women in the world. Read to find out why and how this happens.

Eleanor Roosevelt
by Jane Goodsell

The tall brown house in New York City was quiet. The little girl was almost asleep. Suddenly, she woke with a start. Someone was calling her name.

"Eleanor!" It was her aunt calling from across the hall. "My throat is sore and I have no ice! Would you bring me some from the icebox, please?"

Eleanor caught her breath. The icebox was outside the basement door. It was late at night, and she was afraid of the dark.

She tiptoed down the stairs of the big, gloomy house. She felt her way through the black basement. Her heart beat so fast that she could hardly breathe. But she returned with the ice.

143

Her aunt thanked her, and told her she was a good girl. Eleanor only smiled, but she felt warm and happy inside. People almost never said nice things to her. They were more likely to scold her.

The little girl was very shy, and she didn't smile very often. She wished that she could be cheerful and laugh easily. She longed to be like her mother, who had died when Eleanor was eight. But her mother had been beautiful, and Eleanor knew that she did not look like her mother.

Eleanor had no friends her own age. She spent long hours thinking about her father. She knew that he was dead, but he was still with her in her daydreams. Her father was the only person who had ever made Eleanor feel loved.

Someday, this shy and lonely little girl would have many friends. She would grow up to become the wife of the President of the United States. Her name, Eleanor Roosevelt, would be known to people all over the world.

Now she was ten years old, and she lived in her grandmother's house in New York City. Her four-year-old brother, Hall, lived there, too. So did two of her aunts and two uncles. The rooms were dim and shadowy at night in the light of the gas lamps. Houses did not have electric lights in 1894. There were no cars then, either.

Eleanor's grandmother did not think children needed playmates. Eleanor spent most of her day at lessons in French, music, and sewing. She was not permitted to go outside the house by herself, and she had to take a cold bath every morning. If she was bad, she was sent to bed without supper. Even in summer she had to wear long black stockings. When it was very hot, Eleanor sometimes rolled her stockings to her ankles. But she was quickly told to pull them up. "Ladies do not show their legs!" her grandmother told her.

As Eleanor grew older, she began to go to parties and dances. Her shyness kept her from making friends easily. Often she sat by herself, wishing she were at home reading a book.

But one party was different. A tall and handsome young man asked her to dance. He was Franklin Roosevelt, a distant cousin of Eleanor's.

Franklin danced several dances with Eleanor. He was so friendly that she was not shy. She talked about books she had read and places she had been.

Eleanor and Franklin did not meet again for several years. When Eleanor was fifteen years old, she was sent to a school for girls in England.

The school had strict rules. Beds were made neatly, and dressers kept in perfect order. Eleanor had to study hard. Yet the three years Eleanor spent at the school were the happiest she had known. For the first time she had friends her age.

The headmistress was very kind to Eleanor. She tried to help her get over her shyness. She showed Eleanor how to pick clothes that made her look prettier. She talked to her about books and ideas.

It was a sad day when Eleanor left England to return to her grandmother's house in New York. She dreaded what was ahead. Eleanor was now eighteen years old. At eighteen, the girls in her family entered "society." Almost every evening they went to dances and parties.

Eleanor did not have a good time at dances. Once again she felt shy and lonely. She was bored, too. So many parties seemed silly to Eleanor. She wanted to do something to help other people.

She began to teach dancing and gym to little girls who lived in a slum neighborhood. There was not much fun in these children's lives. But they were happy and giggly as they twirled on their toes in Eleanor's ballet class.

One day Franklin Roosevelt came to the dance class to call for Eleanor. They had now become

good friends. The little girls at the class whispered to Eleanor, "Is he your boyfriend?"

She blushed and said, "Of course not." But the girls guessed right. Franklin loved Eleanor. He asked her to marry him, and she said yes.

Their wedding took place when Eleanor was twenty-one years old. After a trip to Europe they lived in New York City, where Franklin was going to school. He was studying to become a lawyer.

Franklin's mother, Sara Roosevelt, built two houses next door to each other. She lived in one herself. The other she gave to Franklin and Eleanor.

During the next few years Sara Roosevelt ran Eleanor's home. Eleanor did not know how to plan meals and give orders to the workers who cooked and cleaned. Franklin's mother did not help her to learn. Sara Roosevelt wanted to run her son's home herself. She liked being the head of the family.

Eleanor's first child was a little girl. She was named Anna. A boy, James, was born a year later. Franklin's mother hired nurses to take care of the children.

Then Franklin became interested in politics. He was elected to the state Senate. The Senate held its meetings in Albany, the capital of New York State. He and his family moved to Albany.

Now Eleanor was living many miles from Franklin's mother. She had to learn how to run her own home. Eleanor learned then that she could do what had to be done.

After three years in Albany the family moved to Washington, D.C. Franklin had an important job there, working for the Navy. Eleanor and Franklin were invited to parties and gave parties in their own home. Once it would have been very hard for Eleanor to talk to people she did not know. Now she found she could fight her shyness. This was to be true all the rest of her life.

Her family grew. By the time Anna was ten, she had four brothers: James, Elliot, Franklin Junior, and John.

Eleanor did not bring up her children by strict rules. The children called their parents Mom and Pop, and they were seldom punished. Eleanor and Franklin helped with homework. The family played games together. Summers were spent at Campobello, an island off the coast of Maine. There the children had ponies to ride. The family went on picnics and sailed boats on the bay.

At Campobello something happened that changed everything. Franklin had spent the day sailing. When he came home, he felt sick and went to bed. The next morning he had a high fever. Three days later he could not move his legs. He had polio.

For several weeks no one knew if Franklin would live. Franklin did live, but the illness had left his legs very weak. He would have to wear heavy leg braces for the rest of his life. He would never again walk without help.

Yet Franklin made up his mind that he would not spend his life in a wheelchair. His legs were useless, but he could move his arms and shoulders. Each day he exercised to make them stronger.

As Franklin grew better, he talked about the years ahead. What was he going to do with the rest of his life? Eleanor knew then that she must make sure Franklin would go back to politics. It was the most exciting part of his life.

First he must learn to walk with canes and crutches. Until he learned, Eleanor decided, she must keep the Roosevelt name from being forgotten.

Fighting her shyness, she made her first speech. Her voice shook and she giggled nervously. Her second speech was not as hard. Before long she was making speeches around the state. In time she became a very good speaker.

She learned to do other things she had been too timid to try before. She took swimming lessons and learned to drive a car. She went camping with her sons.

Slowly Franklin grew stronger. At last he felt ready to walk with crutches in public. He said that he would make a speech at the Democratic Convention in New York City. He would do it to help a good friend, Alfred E. Smith. Franklin would say that Al Smith should be nominated for President of the United States.

It was very hot in the huge hall the night Franklin made his speech. Eleanor held her breath as he made his way slowly to the speaker's stand. His seventeen-year-old son, Jimmy, walked beside him and held his arm.

The hall was very quiet until Franklin was safely on the platform. Then the crowd stood and cheered him for his courage. Eleanor blinked back tears of pride.

Franklin made a strong and stirring speech about his friend. When he finished, the audience cheered and clapped for a long time. Franklin's speech did not get his friend nominated. But the speech Franklin made became famous. People read about his courage in newspapers. Some said that Franklin Roosevelt would be President someday.

A few years later, Franklin was elected governor of the state of New York. The Roosevelts moved once again to Albany.

Their children were growing up. Anna was married and had children of her own. The boys were away at school.

With her children gone, Eleanor had time to help
Franklin in an important way. Where he could not go
on his crutches, she went in his place. She visited
schools and jails. She learned to look at things
carefully and to ask questions. Sometimes she saw
that buildings were not kept clean. Sometimes she
learned that people were underfed or were not well
treated. She would tell Franklin what she had seen
and heard. Then he would work to make things better.

Franklin was a very good governor. Many people
said that he should become the next President.
Eleanor was not sure she wanted to be the wife of
the President of the United States. It sounded
frightening to her.

Eleanor knew that Franklin would have many
problems if he became the next President. The
United States was in trouble. Millions of people were
out of work and could not find jobs. Many families
had no money at all. Their children were going to
bed hungry.

Yet when Franklin decided to run for President, she helped him every way she could. On election night he won a great victory. He was elected President of the United States.

Eleanor turned out to be a very unusual First Lady. She often walked instead of riding in the Presidential car. She went into the kitchen to scramble eggs for the family. First Ladies usually did not do such things.

Eleanor shook hands with long lines of visitors as she was expected to do. But other things that she did surprised people. She went into dark coal mines to talk with miners. She served soup to hungry men who were out of work. She visited slums. Wherever there were people who needed help, Eleanor Roosevelt went to see what could be done.

All sorts of people were asked to parties at the White House. She invited students, workers, farmers, and fishermen. Of course, many famous people came to the White House, too. Eleanor Roosevelt greeted everyone with the same smile.

Eleanor Roosevelt could never bear to see anyone treated badly. Once, a club refused to let a famous singer, Marian Anderson, sing in its Washington hall. The club did not want her because she was black. Eleanor Roosevelt invited Marian Anderson to sing at the White House. She wanted the world to know that Americans were proud of Marian Anderson.

During the Second World War American soldiers were sent to many parts of the world. Eleanor Roosevelt traveled thousands of miles to visit boys who were far from home and lonely.

Eleanor Roosevelt was loved and admired by millions of people. But some people felt that she should be more dignified. They said she had no business flying all over the world. They called her a busybody. They told jokes about her. She knew what they said, but she had learned that she must do what seemed right to her.

Eleanor Roosevelt lived in the White House twelve years. Franklin was elected President four times. The American people trusted him. They wanted to keep him as their leader. But the long war years were hard on Franklin. He was very thin, and Eleanor knew that he was terribly tired and overworked.

A few months after he began his fourth term as President, Franklin Roosevelt died. His sudden death shocked the world. Eleanor felt lost inside, but she kept her tears to herself. It was she who made others feel better. Her strength helped them to be strong, too.

Now Eleanor was no longer the First Lady. She left the White House for Hyde Park. She moved into a small house because the big house was too large for her now. She wanted to live simply. Most of all, she wanted to be busy and useful.

The war had ended. The United States was on the winning side. But thousands of American boys had been killed. War is sad for winners and losers.

The United Nations was begun in the hope of keeping peace in the world. Its first meeting was held in London in 1946. People from many countries met there.

Eleanor Roosevelt sailed for London as a member of the United States team. She served in the United Nations for six years. She worked for justice and freedom for people everywhere. She helped to write an important paper called the Declaration of Human Rights. When her job ended in 1952, the United Nations had its own building in New York City.

She traveled far and wide. She went to India, Russia, Greece, Turkey, Japan, and many other countries. She spoke for the United Nations. She said it was the world's best hope for peace.

In every country, she met old friends and made new ones. She had become the most famous woman in the world. People felt that she was their friend. Visitors streamed to the little house in Hyde Park to see her. She welcomed kings and queens, presidents, schoolchildren, and neighbors. She liked best of all the times when her own family gathered together. She loved to read stories to her grandchildren and great-grandchildren.

She was seventy-eight years old when she died. Millions of people all over the world wept at the news of her death. The little girl who had no friends had grown up to be known and loved by people everywhere.

Comprehension Check

Think and Discuss

1. What is one important way that Eleanor is different as a grownup than as a child?
2. Why are Eleanor's early years so hard for her?
3. What are three things Eleanor does to help people?
- 4. What is the topic of this selection?
- 5. Which sentence tells the main idea of the first paragraph on page 153?

- Comprehension: Main idea

Communication Workshop

Talk

In some ways, Eleanor is a very unusual person. In other ways, she is like most other people. Get together with your classmates and divide into two groups. One group can discuss some ways that Eleanor stands out. The other group can discuss some ways she fits in. One person can moderate the panel.

Speaking/Listening: Panel discussion

Write

Make a list of some of the things that make Eleanor such an unusual person. Display your list on a bulletin board with your classmates. Notice whether others identified the same traits you did.

Writing Fluency: List

Checking Yourself as You Read

In a few weeks, there will be a contest at the ice rink where you skate. Prizes will be awarded to the best skaters.

You want to win the contest, so you've been practicing your jumps and spins every day after school. You've been checking yourself carefully to see if you're jumping higher and doing better spins.

You can check yourself when you read too. Everyone who reads gets mixed up sometimes. If you check yourself as you read, you can often figure out what you don't understand. Stop and ask yourself:

- Does what I'm reading make sense?
- Do I understand this selection?
- Would it help to read some parts again?
- Are there any words I don't understand? Should I go back and try to figure them out or look them up in a dictionary?

As you read, stop and check. Ask yourself if what you're reading makes sense.

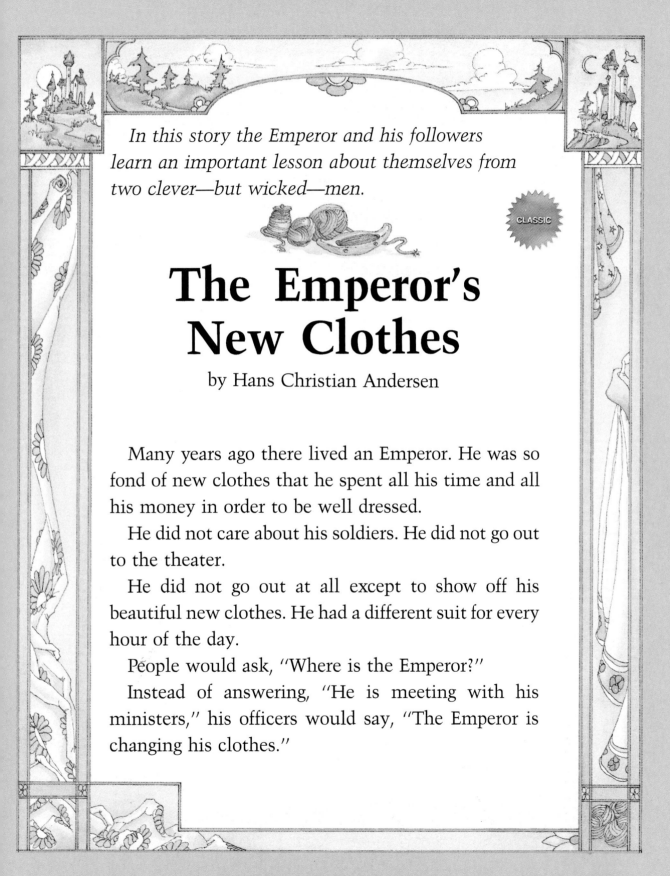

In this story the Emperor and his followers learn an important lesson about themselves from two clever—but wicked—men.

CLASSIC

The Emperor's New Clothes

by Hans Christian Andersen

Many years ago there lived an Emperor. He was so fond of new clothes that he spent all his time and all his money in order to be well dressed.

He did not care about his soldiers. He did not go out to the theater.

He did not go out at all except to show off his beautiful new clothes. He had a different suit for every hour of the day.

People would ask, "Where is the Emperor?"

Instead of answering, "He is meeting with his ministers," his officers would say, "The Emperor is changing his clothes."

Time passed merrily in the city where the Emperor lived.

Visitors came every day.

And one day there came two men who called themselves weavers. But they were really clever rascals.

They pretended that they knew how to weave cloth of the most beautiful colors and designs. And, they said, the clothes made from this magic cloth could be seen only by people who were fit for their jobs, or by people who were very clever.

If a man was not fit for his job, or if he was very stupid, he could not see the beautiful clothes.

"These, indeed, must be splendid clothes!" thought the Emperor. "I must have a suit made of this magic cloth. Then I can find out which men in my kingdom are not good enough for their jobs."

"And I shall be able to tell who is wise and who is foolish. The weavers must make this magic cloth for me."

He gave large sums of money to the weavers and ordered them to begin their work at once.

So the two men who said they were weavers set up two looms. They pretended to work very hard. But really, they did nothing at all.

They asked for silk thread. And they asked for thread made of gold. But they did not use this fine thread. They kept it for themselves.

And then they went on pretending to work until far into the night.

After some time had passed, the Emperor said to himself, "I should like to know how the weavers are getting along with my cloth."

"But I am a little bit worried about going to see it myself. The weavers said that a fool, or a man who is not fit for his job, would not be able to see the cloth."

"I am sure that I am quite safe. But all the same I think it best to send someone else first."

"I will send my faithful old minister to see how the weavers are getting along," said the Emperor. "He will be the best person to see how the cloth looks. He is a wise man, and he is certainly fit for his job."

So the faithful old minister went into the hall where the wicked men were working at empty looms.

"What can be the meaning of this?" thought the old man. And he opened his eyes very wide. "I cannot see any thread on the looms. I cannot see any cloth."

However, he said nothing to the two men.

The men, who were pretending to weave, invited the minister to come nearer.

Then they pointed to the empty looms and asked whether the design pleased him.

"Aren't the colors beautiful?" they said.

The poor old minister looked and looked. But he could not see anything on the looms—and for a very good reason. There was nothing to see!

But of course the minister did not know this. He thought that he must be a foolish man, or not fit for his job.

He looked from side to side and all around. But of course he did not see any cloth. All he could see were the empty looms.

"Dear me," he said to himself, "I must never tell anyone that I could not see the cloth."

"Well, Sir Minister," said one of the weavers, "you do not say whether or not the cloth pleases you."

"Oh! It is most beautiful!" said the minister. "This design, and the colors! Yes, I will tell the Emperor at once what fine cloth you have made!"

"Thank you," said the pretended weavers. Then they named the different colors. The old minister listened carefully so that he could tell the Emperor about the beautiful colors.

And then the wicked men asked for more silk and more gold. "We need more thread to finish the weaving," they said.

Again they were given silk thread and gold thread. And again they kept it all for themselves. They went on pretending to work very hard.

"The work is going very well," the minister told the Emperor. The Emperor was pleased.

Soon after, the Emperor sent an officer of his court to find out when the cloth would be ready.

The officer went to the hall where the weavers were pretending to work.

"Does not the cloth look beautiful?" asked the men.

And they pointed to the empty looms and talked about the designs and colors that were not there.

"I know I am not stupid," thought the officer. "It must be that I am not fit for the very good job I have. That is very strange indeed. However, no one must ever know that I could not see the cloth."

So he talked about the cloth he could not see, saying he was delighted with the colors and the designs.

Then he went to the Emperor and said, "Indeed, Your Majesty, the cloth the weavers are making is very, very beautiful."

The whole city was talking about the splendid cloth which had cost the Emperor so much money.

And now at last the Emperor wanted to go himself to see the beautiful cloth.

He took with him a few of the officers and ministers of the court. Among them were the officer and the minister who had gone to see the cloth before.

As soon as the two weavers heard the Emperor coming, they pretended to work away harder than ever.

But of course the looms were empty!

"Is not the cloth splendid?" said the officer and the minister. "Look, Your Majesty! What a splendid design! What rich colors."

And they pointed to the empty looms. They were sure that everyone else could see the wonderful cloth.

How is this?" said the Emperor to himself. "I can see nothing. This is indeed terrible. Am I a stupid man, or am I not fit to be Emperor? That would be the worst thing that could happen."

Out loud he said, "Oh! The cloth is beautiful. I am delighted with it." And he smiled most charmingly.

The Emperor did not want anyone to know that he could not see the cloth.

All his followers now looked and looked. They were trying to see something on the looms. But they could not see a thing.

However, they all cried, "Oh, how beautiful!" And they advised the Emperor to have a new suit made of this splendid cloth.

"You must have the suit for the great procession tomorrow," they said.

"Splendid! Beautiful! Wonderful!" were said over and over again. Everyone was very gay indeed.

The Emperor pretended to share in the delight of his followers. He gave the two clever rascals the title of Gentlemen Weavers and a royal ribbon to wear in their buttonholes.

The wicked men sat up all night. They had sixteen lights burning, so that everyone could see how hard they were working.

They pretended to roll the cloth off the looms.

They cut the air with their scissors and used needles without any thread in them..

"See!" they cried at last. "The Emperor's new suit is ready!"

And now the Emperor and all his court came to see the weavers' work.

The rascals pretended to hold up the Emperor's new clothes.

"Here are Your Majesty's trousers!" they said.

"Here is the coat! The whole suit is as light as a cobweb!"

Any man wearing it might think that he had nothing on. That however, is the wonderful thing about this magic cloth."

"Yes, indeed!" said all the court. But not one of them could see anything at all.

"If Your Majesty would be pleased to take off your clothes, we will fit on the new suit in front of the mirror."

The Emperor was then undressed, and the rascals pretended to dress him in his new clothes.

The Emperor turned around and around in front of the mirror.

"How splendid His Majesty looks in his new clothes! And how well they fit!" everyone cried.

"What a design! What colors! They are indeed fit for an Emperor!"

"The procession is waiting, Your Majesty," said the officers.

"I am ready," answered the Emperor.

"Do my clothes fit well?" he asked. And he turned around again in front of the mirror. He wanted everyone to think he was admiring his new suit.

The officers who were to carry His Majesty's train felt about on the ground as if they were lifting up the ends. Then they pretended to be carrying something.

They could never for a minute let anyone think that they were stupid or not fit for their jobs.

So now the Emperor walked in the procession, right through the streets of his city.

And all the people standing by and those at the windows cried out, "Oh, how beautiful the Emperor's new clothes are! How well they fit! What a splendid train!"

No one said that he could not see any clothes, for that would mean he was stupid or not fit for his job.

Never before had any of the Emperor's clothes caused so much excitement.

"But the Emperor has nothing on at all!" said a little child.

What the child said was whispered from one to another, until everyone knew.

And they all cried out together, "HE HAS NOTHING ON AT ALL!"

The Emperor felt very silly, for he knew that the people were right. But he thought, "The procession must go on!"

So the Emperor held his head higher than ever. And his officers took even greater trouble to pretend to hold up the train which wasn't there at all.

Meet the Author

Hans Christian Andersen was one of the greatest storytellers of all time. For over one hundred years his unforgettable tales have delighted people of all ages in every corner of the world.

Hans Christian Andersen's own life was like a fairy tale. He was born in Odense, Denmark, in 1805. When he was eleven, his father, a poor shoemaker, died. Andersen left school and went to work. At age fourteen, a tall, skinny boy whose clothing always seemed too small for him, Andersen set off for Copenhagen to find his fortune. He tried ballet, singing, and acting but failed at them all. Finally, one of Andersen's friends talked to the King of Denmark. The King met Andersen, liked him, and gave him money to finish his schooling.

During his school years Andersen began writing stories and plays. His first fairy tale, "The Snow Maiden," appeared in a newspaper.

Many of Andersen's fairy tales are based on things that happened in his own life. The idea for "The Ugly Duckling" came from feelings Andersen had about not belonging when he was young.

Today men, women, and children everywhere know and love Andersen's fairy tales. He is one of the most widely read authors in the world. "The Emperor's New Clothes," "The Little Mermaid," "The Fir Tree,"—which is your favorite?

LOOKING BACK

Thinking and Writing About the Section

The people in this section who learned to "be themselves" had important events in their lives. You can write a news story about one of these events to share with your class. Copy the chart and fill it in.

See your Thinker's Handbook for tips.

Who	What: An Important Event	When, Where, Why
the deaf sister		
Eleanor Roosevelt	gave her first speech	
Emperor		

Writing

Write a news story about one of the events. Include *who*, *what*, *when*, *where*, and *why* it happened. Write a headline to summarize the main idea. If you need more help, see your Writer's Handbook.

Revising

Read your first draft to a partner. Does your headline give the main idea? Did you include the *W* questions? Make changes, proofread, and make a final copy.

Presenting

Contribute your news story to a class newspaper. Help tape the stories to long sheets of paper.

Books to Read

Baby Dinosaurs by Helen Roney Sattler

Did you know that newborn dinosaurs were smaller than human babies? You will learn many new things about baby dinosaurs in this beautifully illustrated book.

The Banza by Diane Wolkstein

In this tale from Haiti, Cabree the goat tries to save herself from ten hungry tigers. Can a musical instrument help her?

Ramona the Pest by Beverly Cleary

Ramona is finally old enough to go to school! She loves school and she loves her teacher. Yet sometimes, just when Ramona is trying her hardest to be good, everything goes wrong.

4

For the Fun of It

Lee Blair wrote this poem for the fun of it.

Raisin Bread

Here is the reply made by Benny
When he was questioned by Lenny:
"Do you like raisin bread?"
"I don't know," Benny said,
"'Cause I never have tried raisin' any."

Have fun! Read a tall tale about an amazing baseball player. Put on a play. Learn how cartoons are made.

"Raisin Bread" from *Funny Folks in Limerick Land* by Leland B. Jacobs. Copyright © 1971 by Leland B. Jacobs. Reprinted with the permission of Garrard Publishing, Champaign, Illinois.

Understanding Fiction and Nonfiction

Two selections you've read are very different from each other. *The Emperor's New Clothes* is a made-up story. The author made up the characters and events. *Chimbuko* is about real animals, people, and events.

A made-up story like *The Emperor's New Clothes* is **fiction.** A fictional story may begin with words like "Once upon a time." It may tell what the characters think and feel. It may have drawings that don't look real.

A selection that gives facts about real people, places, things, and events is **nonfiction.** *Chimbuko* and *Strings Around the World* are nonfiction. Photographs, diagrams, and graphs are often used with nonfiction.

Knowing if a selection is fiction or nonfiction can help you as you read. If you want to read facts about something, pick a nonfictional selection.

Sometimes it is hard to tell if a selection is fiction or nonfiction. The events in *Ty's One-man Band* could have happened, but the drawings don't look real and the author tells what Ty thinks and feels. The story is fiction.

Read the paragraph and decide if it is fiction or nonfiction.

The beach was Lisa's favorite playground. When she swam in the water Lisa thought, I am the queen of the sea and a castle is my home. Lisa carefully built her castle from sand. She dreamed that the shells were her gold coins. "I am a rich but kind queen who will guard the sea from danger," Lisa said to herself. Just then, a wave came and washed away her castle, but Lisa was still the queen of the sea in her dreams.

Answer these questions.

1. Which sentences tell what Lisa thinks and feels? Sentences two, four, and five tell what she thinks and feels.

2. Is this selection fiction or nonfiction? Look at the answer to question 1.

Practicing Fiction and Nonfiction

Read the selection below. Decide if it is fiction or nonfiction.

Tennis

The game of tennis was invented in England in 1873. At that time, the game was called tennis-on-the-lawn or lawn tennis.

Tennis is now played indoors or outdoors. Two or four players play on a court using rackets and balls. If two people play, the game is called singles. If four people play, it is called doubles.

1. Can you check the facts in this selection?
2. Does the author tell what characters think and feel?
3. Is this selection fiction or nonfiction? Why?

Tips for Reading on Your Own

• If the people or events in a selection are made-up, it is fiction.
• If a selection contains facts about people, places, or events, it is nonfiction.

In this funny selection you will read about Florence, a baseball player like no other. Compare the things she does to the things most baseball players do. Then decide if the selection is fiction or nonfiction.

FLEET-FOOTED FLORENCE

by Marilyn Sachs

Matt, the famous baseball hero, had three sons. He hoped that they would become baseball players too.

The first one was named Willie M., after the great hitter. But the only thing Willie M. was great at hitting was his younger brother.

The second one was named Lou B. after the great base stealer. But Lou B. was only great at stealing food from the refrigerator.

The third one was named Johnny B., after the great catcher. But the only thing Johnny B. ever caught was colds.

Matt had a daughter too. He didn't expect *her* to become a baseball player, so he called her Florence N., after the great nurse.

One day, there was a fire a few blocks away from where Matt lived. Matt stood on the porch and watched. First, he saw the fire engines go by. Then he saw the police car go by. Then he watched the neighborhood kids run by. He saw Willie M. and Lou B. and Johnny B. Then he saw a blue whoosh.

"What," he asked a neighbor, "was that blue whoosh?"

"That blue whoosh," said the neighbor, "was your daughter, Florence."

Then Matt knew that his daughter, Florence N., would grow up to be a baseball player.

Matt taught her how to hit. And he taught her
how to catch. He taught her how to throw. But he
did not have to teach her how to run.

When Florence N. grew up, she went to play on her father's old team, The North Dakota Beavers. They had won thirteen World Series in a row in the days Matt played for them. But ever since he left, they had been in a slump.

Florence changed all that. She was the fastest runner in the West and the fastest runner in the East. She was the fastest runner in the North and the fastest runner in the South.

Nobody ever ran as fast as Florence. When she came up to bat, everybody on the other team trembled. Because they knew that once she got on base, if there was nobody in front of her, she would come home.

Her fans called her FLEET-FOOTED FLORENCE, and every game you could hear them shout: HOORAY FOR FLEET-FOOTED FLORENCE!

But her enemies called her FLAT-FOOTED
FLORENCE. Every game, you could hear them
shout: PHOOEY ON YOU, FLAT-FOOTED FLORENCE!

Florence played center field. She could run faster
than the ball. So when she caught it, if there was a
runner trying to advance after the catch, she
usually ran in to tag him out.

She specialized in four outs. Whenever the bases
were loaded, and she caught a fly ball, she liked to
run in and personally tag each player out as he
returned to his base.

Once she tripped over a can flung on the field,
but she played anyway. She stole two bases
instead of three, and put only three men out
instead of four.

She could hop faster than most people could run.
Sometimes when her team was leading, she would
play with one leg tied behind her back.

The North Dakota Beavers won the pennant the first year Florence came to play on their team. And that year, they faced their old enemies, the New York Yankees, in the World Series.

Now the mightiest Yankee of all was Fabulous Frankie, the magnificent catcher. Frankie could catch, and Frankie could hit, and Frankie could throw.

But Frankie could not run as fast as Florence, and Frankie had a habit of hitting balls out toward center field. Florence made more four outers off Frankie's fly balls than anybody else's.

This made Frankie angry—very angry, very, very, angry! So angry, in fact, that he flipped. Every time Florence caught his fly balls or tagged out his teammates, or stole three bases under his nose, he flipped. He flipped so much that he became known as FRANKIE, THE YANKEE FLIPPER.

The worst thing was that he lost his cool. He lost his appetite too, and he lost his sleep. He started letting pitches get by him, and North Dakota Beaver fans began yelling: FUMBLE-FINGERED FRANKIE, THE YANKEE FLIPPER YAA! YAA! YAA! Nobody called him Fabulous anymore.

One day, after the Beavers had won their third
World Series game off the Yankees, and were trying
for their fourth, Florence hit a tiny, baby bunt, and
came flying around the bases into home plate just
as Frankie was picking it up.

They met head on. Eyeball to eyeball. They had
never been so close to one another.

After that, Frankie didn't seem to mind when
Florence made four outs off his fly balls. And
sometimes, Florence even counted to ten before
she ran in and made her four outs.

It was in all the papers.

FLEET-FOOTED FLORENCE FLIPS OVER FABULOUS
FRANKIE

Soon after, they got married.

Frankie was traded to The North Dakota Beavers, and he and Florence became the most famous pair in baseball history. They did live happily ever after too, but that is not the end of the story.

Florence set so many records that there was no book big enough to hold them all. Most great baseball players become famous because of their RBI's* or ERA's** or just their BA's***. Florence, alone, is also famous for being the only player to have an outstanding record of RCI's****.

Of course, she had to make sure each player she carried in touched each base before she did.

*Runs batted in
**Earned run averages
***Batting averages
****Runs carried in

One day, a woman, dressed in a shabby baseball cap and jacket, stood outside the dugout asking for autographs. All the other players hurried by, except for Florence.

She smiled at the woman. She asked about her health. And she autographed her scorecard. "Fleet-footed Florence," said the woman, "you are the greatest baseball star who ever lived."

"Ah," sighed Florence, "I wish I might always be a star."

The woman pulled from under her warm-up
jacket a golden baseball. "Because you are good
and kind as well as a great star, I have it in my
power to grant you your wish."

Then the woman threw the ball with all her
might, and Florence said, "Never fear, I will
retrieve that ball for you."

So saying, she hurried after the glittering ball. Faster and faster it rolled, and faster and faster Florence ran after it. Out of the stadium, through the parking lot, and over the city streets spun the golden ball. Right behind it came Florence, laughing in the joy of the race. And right behind Florence, came Frankie, crying, "Florence, wait for me!"

Suddenly, the ball rose up into the sky, and Florence reached back for Frankie, and leaped.

Florence and Frankie were never seen again. Some say they have retired into the country and are raising a family of future ballplayers—five girls and four boys.

Some say they are traveling incognito, and can be seen scouting every sand lot where future ballplayers are most likely to be found. Maybe so.

But I think you should look carefully up at the sky on a clear night. Do you really think that flashing, glittering light that moves faster than anything else up there is only a shooting star? Watch! Here it comes again, and see, it really is not a shooting star. You know who it really is racing across the sky, carrying Frankie in her arms, flying faster than the moon, faster than the sun, faster than any of the other stars.

Fleet-footed Florence, for all time now, the fastest star in the firmament.

Meet a Reader

When Colleen Fox curls up on her bed to read, she might pick a new book by Eleanor Estes, Judy Blume, or Marilyn Sachs, or she might reread an old favorite like *The Moffats*, *Tales of a Fourth Grade Nothing*, *Superfudge*, *Sleeping Beauty*, or *Cinderella*. These books are her favorites because Colleen can put herself in the main character's place. Sometimes she imagines that she *is* a character from a book she's reading.

One reason Colleen likes *Fleet-footed Florence* is that she thinks the main character is interesting. Colleen says, "If Florence were real, I'd like to meet her."

Colleen enjoyed reading about Florence and Frankie getting married, and she liked the ending of the book very much. Colleen thought the description of Florence as a "blue whoosh" was funny.

If you visit Colleen at her home in Wisconsin, you might find her riding a bike, swimming, or playing with her dolls or her bead collection. Then again, you might find her rereading *Fleet-footed Florence*.

Comprehension Check

Think and Discuss

1. What are some things Florence does that no other baseball player can do?
2. When does Matt first know that his daughter will grow up to be a baseball player?
3. Why does Frankie change after he meets Florence eyeball to eyeball?
 • 4. Is *Fleet-footed Florence* fiction or nonfiction? Why?
5. Think of the best baseball player you know. In what way is that player like Florence and in what way is the player different?

See your Thinker's Handbook for tips.

 • Comprehension: Fiction and nonfiction

Communication Workshop

Talk

What if Florence was a basketball player instead? What sort of special stunts might she do on her way to the basket? Get together with a group of classmates. Take turns role-playing things that Florence might do.

Speaking/Listening: Role-playing

Write

Write a paragraph describing a basketball game in which Florence played. Contribute your paragraph to a class scrapbook that tells about Florence's games!

Writing Fluency: Paragraph

You may laugh at some of the foolish things Juan says,
but how foolish is he really? Compare what you think about
Juan at the beginning of the play with what you think
about him at the end.

Juan Bobo and the Queen's Necklace

A Puerto Rican Folk Tale Told by Pura Belpré
Stage Adaptation by Nina Shengold

CHARACTERS

THE QUEEN	THE KING'S SERVANT
HER THREE MAIDS	JUAN BOBO
(MARIA, PIA, and ROSALITA)	OLD PEASANT
THE KING	JUAN'S MOTHER
BIRTHDAY GUESTS	THE COOK

SCENE ONE: *The Queen's Bedroom*

(The QUEEN *lies in her bed. Her three maids,* MARIA, PIA, *and* ROSALITA, *come in carrying breakfast on big silver trays.)*

ALL THREE MAIDS: Good morning, Your Majesty.

MARIA: We wish you a marvelous birthday!

PIA: A wonderful birthday!

ROSALITA: A *terrible* birthday!

QUEEN: What?

MARIA: Rosalita, you silly goose, why do you say the wrong word all the time?

ROSALITA: I don't know.

PIA: We're sorry, Your Majesty, our little sister meant to say *terrific.*

ROSALITA: That's right! I did! I meant *terrific!*

PIA: Rosalita is new in the palace. We're sure she will learn very quickly. She already knows how to carry a tray. See how well she serves breakfast?

(The MAIDS *serve the* QUEEN.*)*

QUEEN: What's this?

(She points to a velvet box on one of the trays.)

MARIA: That's a gift from the King. Happy birthday!

(The QUEEN opens the box. Inside is a beautiful, shiny pearl necklace.)

QUEEN: Look! Aren't they beautiful? See how they shine in the sunlight! I've never seen such beautiful pearls. I can't wait to get dressed for the dance tonight! I'll be the star of the ballroom! I love having birthdays! I love getting gifts! I love being Queen!

ALL THREE MAIDS: Yes, Your Majesty.

SCENE TWO: *The Palace Ballroom*

(Late that night. Music plays as the KING *and* QUEEN *dance. There are many guests watching and clapping. The* QUEEN *wears her pearl necklace.)*

QUEEN: This was the best birthday I've ever had.

KING: Really? What was your favorite part? Was it breakfast in bed? Or the cook's special banquet? The play that your ladies-in-waiting put on for you?

QUEEN: No. It was my new pearls.

KING: Ah!

QUEEN: I like the way everyone stares at them.

SCENE THREE: *The King's Throne Room*
(The next morning. The KING sits on his throne reading a scroll. His SERVANT runs in, out of breath.)

SERVANT: Your Highness.

KING: Be quiet, I'm reading the newspaper.

SERVANT: But Your Majesty.

KING: Hush! I said QUIET!

SERVANT: The Queen's pearls are gone!

KING: What? Why didn't you say so?

SERVANT: I did. I just did!

KING: This is terrible. Search the whole palace! Search high and low! Search the guests, the dancers, the ladies-in-waiting, the cook and the guards! Don't stop your search until that necklace is back on the Queen's royal neck! Do you understand?

SERVANT: Yes, Your Highness.

(The SERVANT starts to leave.)

KING: Wait! I have a better idea. Go to the town square and tell all the peasants I'll give a reward to anyone who finds the Queen's pearls.

SERVANT: Yes, Your Highness.

KING: Well, what are you waiting for? GO!

(The SERVANT *runs out.)*

SCENE FOUR: *The Town Square*

*(*PEASANTS *are buying and selling their goods. In
a corner,* JUAN BOBO *sits strumming his guitar and
singing.)*

JUAN BOBO: *My name is Juan Bobo*
They say I'm a dodo
Or some kind of yoyo
But I tell them no, no I'm not. . . .

(The King's SERVANT *runs in, even more out of breath.)*

SERVANT: Attention! Attention! The Queen's new pearls are gone! The pearls are gone! The King will reward anyone who can find them!

OLD PEASANT: How much is the reward?

SERVANT: A lot!

JUAN *(aside, to his* MOTHER): Mother, did you hear that? I want to find those pearls. Then we could share the reward and we'd always have food on the table.

JUAN'S MOTHER: Juan, my son, you are a bobo. A bobo can't find things. Leave that to the smart people.

JUAN: Mother, I want to try. Give me your blessing.

JUAN'S MOTHER: You always have my blessing, Juan, you know that. But blessings won't keep you from being a bobo. You just stare off in space and strum your guitar all day long. How could that help you find anything?

JUAN: I don't know, but I want to try.

(JUAN *slings his guitar on his shoulder and goes up to the King's* SERVANT.)

JUAN: Excuse me, but I'd like to look for the Queen's pearls.

SERVANT: Excuse *me*, but aren't you Juan Bobo, the most foolish fellow in the land?

JUAN: I don't know.

SERVANT *(aside)*: He doesn't know! That's pretty foolish! *(to* JUAN *slyly):* How much is one plus one?

JUAN: Three.

SERVANT: Ha! You must be Juan Bobo, you dodo!

JUAN: One pair of shoes plus one hat—that makes three.

(The SERVANT *counts his shoes and hat.)*

SERVANT: One pair of shoes . . . one, two . . . plus my hat—that's three! *(aside)*: Maybe he's not such a bobo!

SERVANT *(to* JUAN): Come, try your luck!

JUAN: Thank you.

(They leave.)

SCENE FIVE: *The King's Throne Room*

SERVANT: Your Majesty, this is Juan Bobo. He has come to look for the Queen's pearls.

KING: What kind of a name is Juan Bobo? This man must be a dodo!

SERVANT: Don't be too sure. He can count to three.

KING: Everyone else has searched. Why shouldn't a bobo try? Welcome, Juan.

JUAN: Thank you, Your Majesty.

KING: Servant, show Juan to a room. And make sure those three silly maids fix it up nicely.

SERVANT: I will, Your Majesty.

SCENE SIX: *A Small Room in the Palace*

SERVANT: Here is your room.

JUAN: Listen! Nightingales!

(JUAN *runs to the window and looks down into the
     courtyard garden.*)

JUAN: Do you hear them?

SERVANT: I hear some birds making noise, that's all.

(SERVANT *goes out.*)

JUAN: Those are nightingales singing. Now, how
     many are there? I can hear one, two . . . three
     of them! I love to hear nightingales singing.
     That's much more important than looking for
     pearls. I will play my guitar for them.

(JUAN *sits by the window and starts to make up a tune.*)

JUAN: *Where are you, nightingales?*
     Where can you be?
     I'm looking for one, two
     I'm looking for three!

(MARIA *and* PIA *come in carrying blankets and sheets. Just then two nightingales fly past the window.*)

JUAN: *There you go, there you are*
Oh, lucky me
I've spotted the first pair
That's two out of three!

MARIA & PIA: What?

(MARIA *and* PIA *drop the bedding and run out of the room.*)

JUAN: That's funny. What silly maids!

(JUAN *looks back out the window.*)

JUAN: I still hear one nightingale singing. What a beautiful voice she has! I wonder where she could be hiding?

(*He plays his guitar again.*)

JUAN: *Where are you, nightingale?*
Sweet singing bird
I've seen your two sisters
Now I see the third!

(ROSALITA *enters Juan's room with a tray of food. She hears the last lines of his song.*)

ROSALITA: What? Oh no! (*She drops tray and runs out of room.*)

JUAN: Where did they get these maids? I'm a bobo, but I can make beds and serve lunch without dropping things!

(*The* THREE MAIDS *come back in, shaking with fear.*)

MARIA: How did you know we had done it?

JUAN: Done what?

PIA: Don't pretend to be foolish. How did you catch us?

JUAN: I didn't.

ROSALITA: Nobody else figured out that we took the pearl necklace, but you picked us out one, two, three. How did you do it, Juan Bobo?

JUAN: Why, I was just sitting and singing and counting the nightingales.

MARIA: Don't make jokes. Please help us!

PIA: We want to return the Queen's necklace. We're sorry we took it.

MARIA: You can't imagine how sorry we are. We feel horrible!

PIA: Awful!

ROSALITA: *Terrific!*

MARIA: She did it again! Rosalita means *terrible*.

ROSALITA: That's right! I feel *terrible*.

PIA: What can we do?

MARIA: Help us, Juan Bobo!

JUAN: Why don't you just give the pearls back?

MARIA: The Queen will be angry. We're frightened!

PIA: Afraid!

ROSALITA: *Fearless!*

MARIA: Oh, come on, Rosalita.

ROSALITA: I'm sorry. I get so confused.

PIA: She means *fearful.*

JUAN: Rosalita knows lots of good words. Now, let me help you. Before it is light tomorrow, go to the barnyard. Drop the pearls into the bucket of corn near the biggest goose. Then leave the rest to me.

ALL THREE MAIDS: We will. Thank you, Juan!

SCENE SEVEN: *The King's Throne Room*

(The next day. JUAN *bows before the King.)*

JUAN: Good news, Your Highness.

KING: You've found the pearl necklace?

JUAN: Yes and no. I don't have the necklace, but I know where it is. To get it you must eat a goose for dinner, and not just any goose but the biggest one in the barnyard.

KING *(to his* SERVANT*):* Call in the cook.

The COOK *enters and bows.*

KING: I want the biggest goose in the barnyard for dinner tonight. Go now to choose the goose! Juan will help you.

(The COOK *and* JUAN *go out running.)*

SCENE EIGHT: *The Palace Kitchen*

(*The* COOK *prepares the goose.*)

COOK: First the King wants a tender lamb for dinner. Then he wants a goose. Why can't he make up his mind? Wait! What's this?

(*As the* COOK *cuts open the goose, the Queen's necklace pops out.* JUAN *picks up the necklace and rushes away with it.*)

SCENE NINE: *The King's Throne Room*

(JUAN *enters holding the pearl necklace.*)

KING: The necklace! Juan, I don't know how a bobo like you could find it. But here it is.

(*The* QUEEN *and the* THREE MAIDS *enter.*)

QUEEN: My pearls! My beautiful pearls!

(*She puts on the necklace and everyone cheers.*)

KING: Name your reward, Juan. Would you like to ask a lady-in-waiting to marry you?

JUAN: No, sir. I would rather bring food to my poor mother.

KING: You shall have all the food you want, Juan Bobo.

ROSALITA: He isn't a bobo!

JUAN (*looks at* ROSALITA): Can I ask Rosalita to marry me *and* have some food?

KING: Of course! Let there be dancing!

(JUAN *takes* ROSALITA's *hand, the* KING *takes the* QUEEN's, *and the* SERVANT *takes* MARIA's. JUAN's MOTHER *comes in with the* OLD PEASANT *and they all start to dance.*)

Comprehension Check

Think and Discuss

1. Do you think Juan is foolish? Why or why not?
2. How does Juan discover who has the necklace?
3. Why do you think Juan helps return the necklace to the Queen?
4. How is Rosalita like Maria and Pia? How is she different?
- 5. Use one of these words to complete each analogy.
   wonderful   white   bad   dress
   a. Ruby is to red as pearl is to _____.
   b. Terrific is to terrible as good is to _____.

- Comprehension: Comparisons (analogy)

Communication Workshop

Talk

If you were putting on the play *Juan Bobo and the Queen's Necklace*, what would you tell the actors about the characters? Get together with a partner and discuss the traits of each character.

Speaking/Listening: Cooperative learning

Write

Describe one character from the play to help the actor of that part know how to read the lines. Tell what the character will wear and use. Read your description to the actor who plays that part.

Writing Fluency: Description

A Quick Look Ahead

You are playing checkers with a friend. It is your turn to move. You look at all the places on the board. You know you must look ahead and plan your moves carefully to play well.

Before you read a selection, you can do some things that will help you read well. Flip through the pages of the selection quickly. Read the title and any headings that are used. Look at the pictures. Doing this will give you an idea what the selection is about before you read it. This way of looking ahead is called **previewing.**

Let's preview a selection from this book. Turn to the selection that begins on page 243. As you preview, ask yourself these questions:

- What is the selection about?
- What do the pictures show?
- What might I learn from this selection?

Preview to get a quick idea of what a selection is about before you go back and read it.

Why do people have fun making and watching animated films? One reason is that animation can show things that can't happen in real life. As you read about animation, notice the facts and opinions in the article.

Animation

by Marianne von Meerwall

Welcome to the world of animation—a world where fish can laugh and tables can fly. It's a place where a dot can grow into an elephant and a piece of clay can catch a truck and chew it up.

Animation is the art of movement. To make an animated film, artists make a group of drawings. Then they animate them, or make them seem to move. Animation can make things move in ways they can't move in real life. Animation can make things that are not alive seem to be living.

An animated cartoon is made up of many tiny pictures. Each picture is called a *frame*. Each frame is a little bit different from the one before it.

To make an animated cartoon of a person walking, for example, a great many pictures must be drawn. The first drawing may show the person with both feet on the ground. In the drawings that follow, the left foot comes up. Next, the left foot comes down as the right foot comes up. Then the right foot meets the left foot so that the person's feet are together. Finally, the person begins another step. All these drawings last for only a second or two in a film. To show a person walking, a set of pictures must be repeated many times.

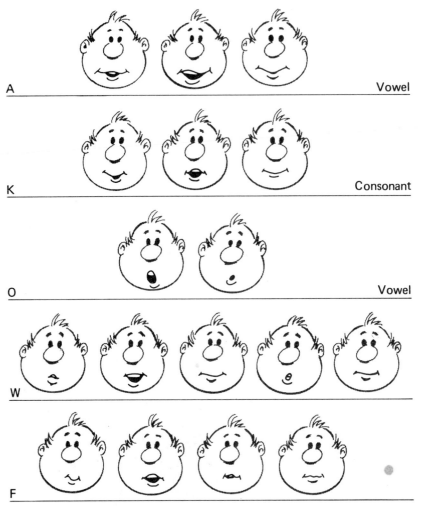

A _____ Vowel

K _____ Consonant

O _____ Vowel

W _____

F _____

Animated cartoons show smiling, frowning, and talking characters. Many different drawings may be needed to show the lip movements for just one sound. Some letter sounds, such as *a* and *k*, are shown by a simple open mouth. For other letter sounds, such as *o*, *w*, and *f*, the drawings must be more exact. People who draw cartoons often act out smiles, frowns, and lip movements in front of a mirror as they draw. This helps them make their characters' faces and lips move in a way that seems real.

In an animated cartoon there may be dozens of characters making many movements. Each of those movements needs a set of drawings.

After the drawings are finished, they are traced onto clear plastic. Then colors are painted on. Finally, the drawings are photographed frame by frame. When the film is shown on a movie screen, the frames go by so fast that the drawings seem to move.

Teams of people work closely together to make an animated cartoon. Each person has a job to do. Each job has to be done well to make a good cartoon. Even with many people working, a two-hour cartoon may take as long as two or three years to finish.

The most famous animator, or artist who draws movie cartoons, was Walt Disney. Some people believe that he is the best animator who ever lived. Disney's first cartoons starred Mickey Mouse. People all over the world have come to know and love Mickey and Disney's other cartoon characters, Minnie Mouse, Donald Duck, Goofy, Pluto, Bambi, Dumbo, and Snow White.

Walt Disney created many of our favorite cartoon characters. But he didn't draw all of the cartoons for every Disney film. After he drew Mickey Mouse for his early cartoons in the 1920s and 1930s, Disney himself did little drawing. Other people in his studio drew, and he thought up the ideas. That was Walt Disney's greatest talent—dreaming up wonderful ideas, figuring out how to make them work, and finding talented people to help him.

There are many other ways to make an animated film besides drawing each frame as the animators at the Walt Disney Studios first did. One way is to use puppets. The puppets are set up against a background. Then they are photographed one frame at a time. After each frame, or after a few frames, the puppets are moved a little bit. When the film is shown, the puppets seem to move.

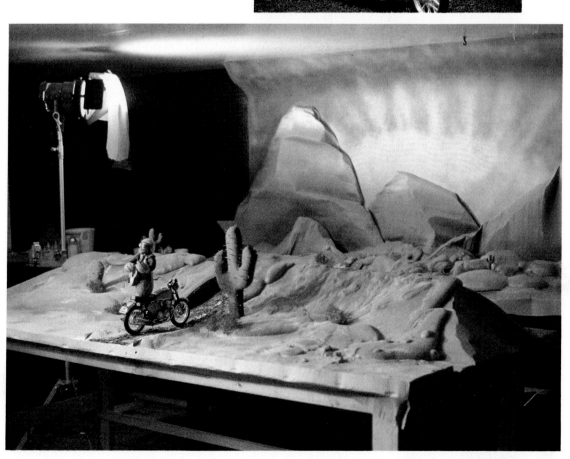

Cutouts can be animated the same way. The main characters are cut out of a paper or cloth. A background is painted on a large piece of paper and put flat on a low table. The cutout characters are put on the background.

A movie camera is pointed down at the characters. A few frames are shot. Then the cutout characters are moved a little bit. Then a few more frames are shot.

Clay has been used to make animated films. It takes only a push or pull to change the shape of a clay character. With clay, one shape can quickly be turned into another. A head can turn into a hand. The hand can turn into a spider then turn into a bird that flies away.

Toys or other real things can also be used to make films. Blocks can fall over each other or build themselves into buildings. Toy planes can seem as if they are flying under the water. Wind-up toys can march through toy cities.

Shots of people can be animated just as puppets and toys are. This is done by photographing a few frames of a person in one position. Then the person changes his or her position and a few more frames are shot. Animation can make people seem to move about in ways that are different from the way they really move. They may seem to do things that they could never do in real life. They may walk through the air or rest their bodies on one finger. They may even clean a whole house from top to bottom in a few seconds.

Some of the most exciting changes in the world of animation have come about through the use of computers. When artists use computers to make animated films, they can show in a short time what would take months or even years to draw frame by frame. A computer can show objects from different points of view. It can show images doing things that would be too hard for a person to draw.

What kind of pictures can be created with a computer? A computer can create almost any kind you can think of. A computer can be used to make animated films that look like things you see in real life. Or it can make films that don't look like anything you've ever seen before.

A spaceship can roar from star to star. Cars can race through the mountains. A bird can fly around a tree and down over a stream. All these things can take place on the screen of a computer. Then they can be put onto film.

You can see computer animation on television every day. Besides cartoon shows, computers are used for weather maps and commercials.

Many of the words that you see on television are animated. The names of television programs and the people who make them are animated by computer. Computers can make words turn over and around so that they are seen in new ways. Words can pop up, change color, and even change shape.

Examples of computer animation

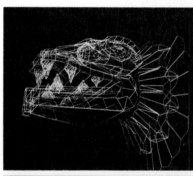

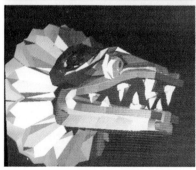

Most animated films have been made by adults. But people as young as eight or nine have made some wonderful animated films.

What equipment would you need if you wanted to make an animated film? A young film maker using some of the equipment you would need is shown on this page.

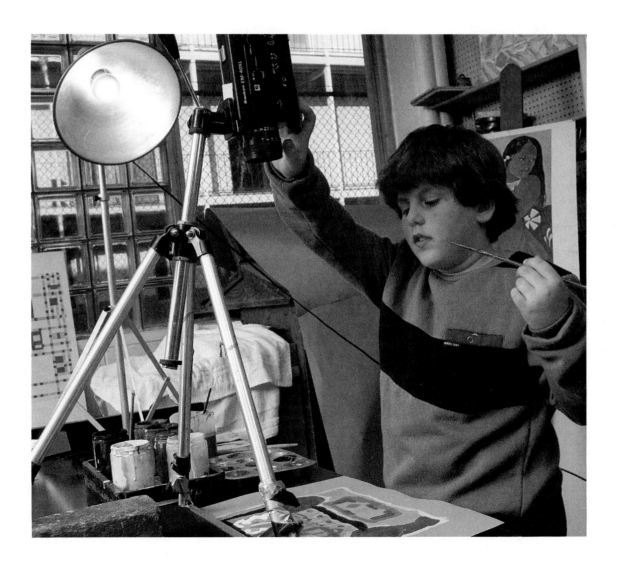

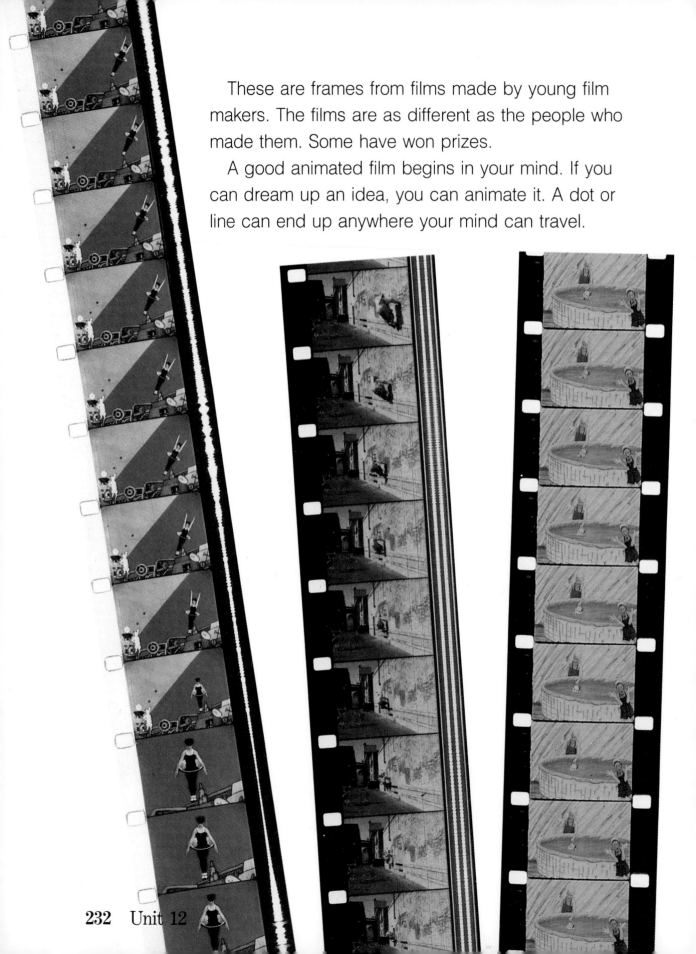

These are frames from films made by young film makers. The films are as different as the people who made them. Some have won prizes.

A good animated film begins in your mind. If you can dream up an idea, you can animate it. A dot or line can end up anywhere your mind can travel.

Comprehension Check

Think and Discuss

1. What are some things animation shows that can't happen in real life?
2. Which do you think would be easier to animate, puppets or clay figures? Why?
- 3. "Disney was the best animator who ever lived." Is this a statement of fact or of opinion? How do you know?
- 4. "After the drawings are finished, they are traced onto clear plastic." Is this a statement of fact or of opinion? How do you know?
5. If you could help make an animated film, would you rather write, draw, or run the camera? Why?

- Comprehension: Fact and opinion

Communication Workshop

Talk

Would you use clay figures or paper cutouts to make an animated film? Discuss the advantages and disadvantages of both with a partner.

Speaking/Listening: Discussion

Write

Write a paragraph for an animated film about a monster who lives at school, a pioneer family, or a bicycle race. Read it to your partner.

Writing Fluency: Paragraph

Unit 12 233

Children in many countries jump rope for fun.
Here are some rhymes that you can hear today and
some that children long ago liked.

Jump-Rope Rhymes

I dreamed that my horse had wings
   and could fly,
I jumped on my horse and rode to the sky.
The man in the moon was out that night,
He laughed loud and long when I pranced
   into sight.

In the *dark dark* world
There's a *dark dark* country
In the *dark dark* country
There's a *dark dark* wood

In the *dark dark* wood
There's a *dark dark* house
And in the *dark dark* house
There is a man trying to mend a fuse!

I asked my mother for fifteen cents,
To see the elephant jump the fence,
He jumped so high.
He reached the sky,
And didn't come back till the Fourth of July.

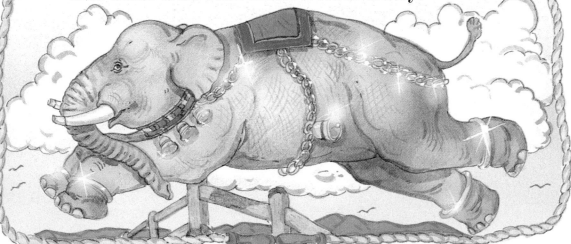

As I was going to Strawberry Fair,
Singing buttercups and daisies
I met a maiden taking the air—
Her eyes were blue and gold her hair,
As she goes on to Strawberry Fair.

Way down south where bananas grow,
The ant stepped on an elephant's toe
Then the elephant cried with tears in his eyes,
Why don't you pick on somebody your size?

LOOKING BACK

Thinking and Writing About the Section

See your Thinker's Handbook for tips.

Prewriting

In this section, you read about things people do for fun. Which do *you* think is the best way to have fun? You can write a persuasive paragraph that convinces others to try it. First, copy and fill in this chart.

Selection	How You Can Have Fun	Reasons Why It Is Fun
"Fleet-Footed Florence"		
"Animation"	writing, drawing a cartoon	

Writing

Use one of the ways to have fun that you listed above to write a persuasive paragraph that convinces others it is fun. Start with a topic sentence that gives your opinion. Give at least two reasons. See your Writer's Handbook if you need more help.

Revising

Read your first draft to a partner. How convincing are your reasons? Make changes and proofread. Then write a final copy.

Presenting

Read your paragraph aloud to the class. Take a vote to find out if you have convinced them.

5

Mysteries

The world is filled with mysteries. Detectives solve some of them. Scientists solve others. Here's a mystery for you. Seven letters are hidden in this picture. The letters spell a word. Can you find all the letters and figure out what the word is?

In this Section you'll find out how Miss Mallard, a crime-fighting duck, solves a puzzling mystery. You'll also read about two mysteries that scientists have begun to solve.

Using Maps and Globes

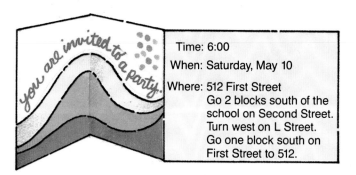

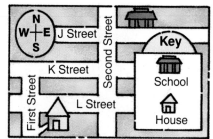

If you were invited to a party, you might receive an invitation like the one on the left. The directions explaining how to get to the party might be hard for you to understand. Perhaps a **map**, a special kind of picture showing a real place, could help you.

Look at the map on the right. It shows you where the birthday party is being held. You can use it to find the house.

The **key** on a map shows what the pictures on the map stand for. Find the picture on the map that stands for the school. Then find the picture that stands for the house where the party will be. The direction arrows on a map show which is north, south, east, and west.

A **globe** is like a map of the earth but it is round, not flat. Globes show the whole world. Do you have a globe in your classroom?

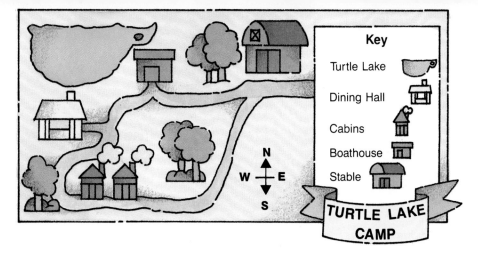

Read the paragraph about Turtle Lake Camp.

It was Jan and Lisa's first day at camp. At breakfast in the dining hall their teacher handed the girls a map and told them to walk around the camp. He said, "See if you can solve the mystery of why the lake is called Turtle Lake."

Use the key and the direction arrows to answer the questions about the map.

1. Should Jan and Lisa walk north or south to get from the dining hall to Turtle Lake? To answer this question place your finger on the dining hall. Then move it to Turtle Lake. The direction arrows show that the girls must go north to get to Turtle Lake.

2. Imagine that Jan and Lisa are at the stables. Which buildings are closer—the cabins or the boathouse? Find the stables on the map. You can see that the boathouse is closer than the cabins.

3. Why is the lake called Turtle Lake? (Turn the map upside down.)

Practicing Using Maps

Mary and Didi invited the new girl at school, Alice, to visit their secret hideout in the park. Help Alice find her way around town using the map Mary and Didi gave her.

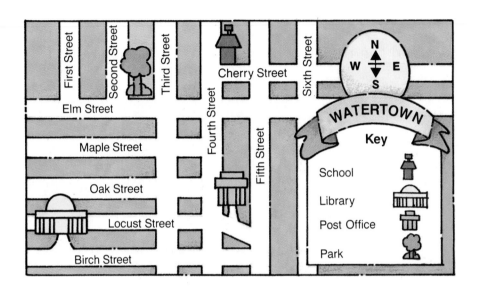

1. The school is at the corner of which streets?
2. Should Alice go east or west to get from the school to the park?
3. After visiting the hideout in the park, the girls are going to the library. Which way will they walk—north or south?

Tips for Reading on Your Own

- Remember that the key tells what the pictures on a map stand for.
- Remember that the direction arrows show which way is north, south, east, and west.

Read about a mystery that has not yet been completely solved. What can a map show you about this mystery?

The Mystery of Disease

by Charnan Simon

All of a sudden it hits. You go to bed one night feeling fine. When you wake up the next morning, your head hurts. Your stomach hurts. Your throat hurts. You have a fever and you ache all over. What is wrong with you?

fever (fē′vər), a body temperature that is greater than normal.

Your grandmother says you caught the flu from walking home in the rain. Getting wet and chilled can make you uncomfortable, but can it make you sick?

Your parents say it is just that time of year. They say the coming of winter signals the coming of flu.

The doctor says you probably picked the flu up from one of your friends. She says that if you take care of yourself, your fever and aches will disappear in a few days. Then you'll feel fine again.

But you still think the mystery is unsolved. What has happened to your body? How did you get sick?

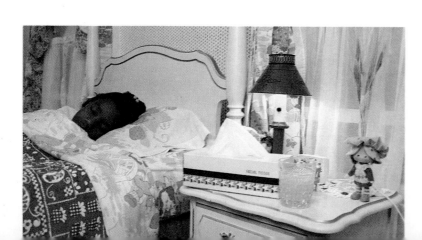

What Is Disease?

Your grandmother, your parents, and the doctor were telling you that you had a sickness or **disease.** The flu normally isn't dangerous if you do what the doctor tells you. Some diseases are dangerous. You can even die from some diseases.

Germs That Cause Infectious Disease

There are many different causes of disease. One cause is **germs.** A germ is a tiny living thing. Germs are found everywhere—in air, in water, and in dirt. They live on your body and in your body. They are so small you need a microscope to see them.

microscope (mī′krə skōp), an instrument that makes small things look larger.

Most germs don't hurt you, but some kinds of germs cause disease. A disease caused by germs is called an **infectious disease.**

Each infectious disease is caused by one kind of germ. To cause a disease, germs must first get in your body. Once inside, germs live, grow, and reproduce. When there are many disease germs in your body, your body can't work the way it should. Then you start to feel sick.

Scientists have learned that different kinds of germs cause infectious diseases. The two most common kinds are **bacteria** and **viruses.**

cell (sel), the very small part of living things of which all plants and animals are made.

Bacteria Bacteria are living things made up of just one cell. Some bacteria cause diseases.

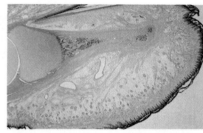

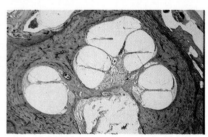

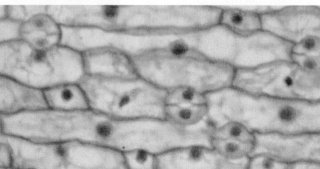

All living things are made of cells like these.

Photographs top/bottom left: Carolina Biological Supply Company

As you can see in the photos, bacteria come in different shapes and sizes.

Viruses   Viruses cause more diseases than bacteria do. They are much smaller than bacteria. A very strong microscope is needed to see viruses.

Common Infectious Diseases

Many different infectious diseases make people sick. Colds, flu, measles, chicken pox, and strep throat are just a few of them.

Did You Know?
Measles and chicken pox are often called children's diseases, because children are most likely to get them.

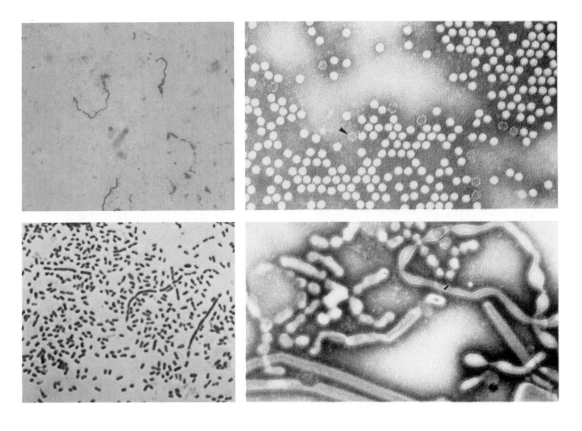

bacteria   viruses

Flu and Colds   Did you know that every time you have the flu, you may get sick in a different way? The reason for this is because there are many different viruses that cause flu.

The same thing is true for colds. There are more than one hundred different viruses that cause colds. With some colds your throat may hurt, and you may cough. With others your nose may run, and you may sniff and sneeze. You may feel chilled with a cold, or your body may ache. Colds are very common diseases. Both adults and children often get colds.

Three Other Diseases   **Chicken pox** is another infectious disease caused by a virus. You have a fever and a headache with chicken pox. With chicken pox your body is covered with red spots called a **rash.** You may want to scratch those spots, but if you do the rash will spread. So hands off!

Measles is also caused by a virus. With measles you have a fever and a cough. Your nose may run, and your eyes are red. You get a rash when you have measles.

There is one good thing about chicken pox and measles. You cannot get them many times the way you can get colds and flu.

Strep throat is an infectious disease that is caused by bacteria. With strep throat you may have a fever, and your throat may hurt—a lot! Strep throat is a common disease, but it can be dangerous. You should see a doctor when you have strep throat. The doctor can give you medicine to cure this disease.

How Infectious Diseases Spread

Most infectious diseases can spread from person to person. The germs that cause the diseases can travel from one person to another. This can happen in several ways.

People Spread Germs   When a sick person coughs or sneezes, germs get in the air. Another person may breathe in the germs. Then that person may get sick.

Germs can get on a tissue, cup, or other thing that a sick person uses. The germs can live there a short time. If another person touches these things, that person may get sick too.

Germs in Water and Food Some germs can travel in water or food. They can live there a short time. People who drink the water or eat the food may get sick.

You can help yourself stay healthy by drinking only water that is clean and free of germs. Water that comes into your house is safe to drink. Water in lakes and streams may not be.

Foods can carry germs too. Washing fruits and vegetables helps remove the germs. Cooking foods such as meat kills most germs that live in the food. Keeping foods such as milk cold helps prevent germs from growing.

malaria
(mə ler′ ē ə), a disease whose signs are chills, fever, and sweating.

Did You Know?
The word *malaria* came from the Italian words *mala aria* meaning "bad air." Before people knew about germs, they thought malaria was caused by breathing bad air near swamps.

Animals and Insects   Animals can carry disease germs. Always wash your hands after you touch an animal. Try to stay away from sick animals.

Insects sometimes carry disease germs. You can get sick if the insect bites you. For example, the germ that causes malaria is carried by certain mosquitoes. People who live near warm, wet places such as swamps often get malaria, because that's where many mosquitoes live.

Another disease carried by an insect is Rocky Mountain spotted fever. This disease is caused by a germ that is bigger than a virus but smaller than a bacteria. The germ is carried by a tiny insect called a wood tick. With this disease there is fever, a rash, and body aches.

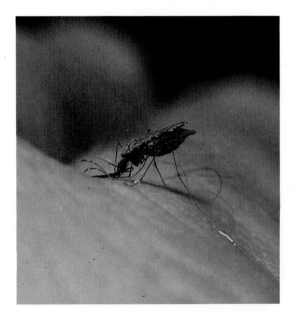
mosquito

wood tick

Rocky Mountain spotted fever got its name in an interesting way. Many years ago pioneers crossing the Rocky Mountains got sick with a new disease. Because they got spots and a fever, they named the disease Rocky Mountain spotted fever. They thought you could only catch the disease in the Rocky Mountains. Now we know that you can catch the disease in other places too. The map below shows where Rocky Mountain spotted fever was first found.

Rocky Mountain States

How Your Body Fights Disease

Your body has ways of keeping germs out. Your skin is a good cover for your body. Germs cannot get through your skin unless you have a cut. Germs *can* get in through your nose and mouth. But hairs and **mucus** in your nose and **saliva** in your mouth help keep germs from traveling any farther.

Some germs do get in your body no matter how hard it works to keep them out. Then your body fights to kill these germs. For example, you have cells in your blood called **white blood cells.** White blood cells surround and kill disease germs in your body. When you get sick, your body makes more white blood cells than normal. They may come from all over your body to fight germs.

Your body also fights germs with fever. Some germs can't live when it is hot. So fever kills these germs. A fever shows that your body is fighting back against disease. A fever that goes too high or lasts too long can be dangerous to your body, though.

Medicines That Kill Germs   Your doctor can give you certain medicines that kill bacteria. These medicines can cure diseases that are caused by bacteria. Most viruses cannot be killed by medicines, though. When you have a disease caused by a virus, your body must work on its own to make you well.

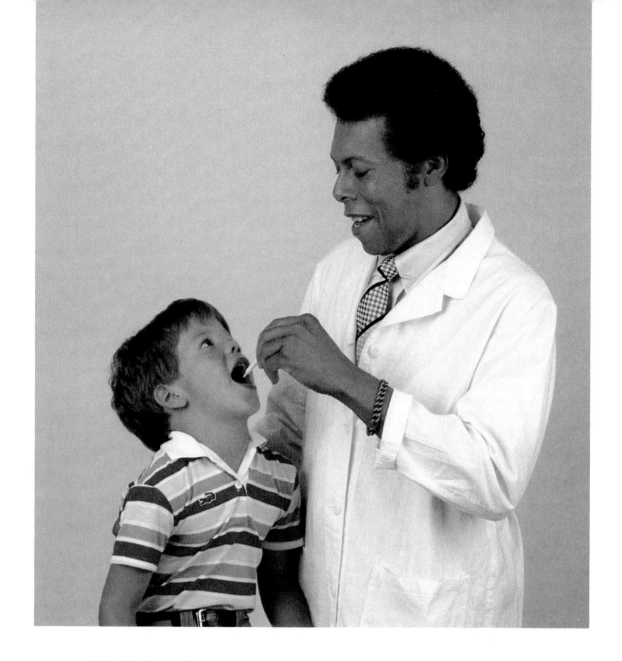

Medicines That Make You Feel Better   Some medicines you can get from your doctor can help you feel better while you are sick. Some medicines can slow down a runny nose. Others can keep you from coughing so hard. These medicines don't cure disease. What they do is make you feel better while your body fights disease germs.

How to Prevent Disease

You have learned how your body fights germs and how doctors can help you when you're sick. Here are some precautions you can take to stay healthy.

Staying Strong   First, you can eat the right foods. You can get enough rest. You can exercise every day. This will keep your body strong and healthy. Then your body will be better able to fight germs. Even if you get sick, you won't get as sick as a person who doesn't have a strong body.

Strong bodies can fight disease germs.

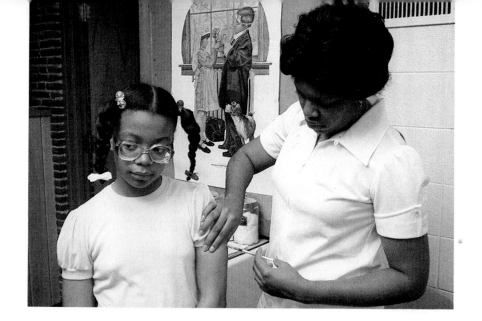

Getting Vaccines   Getting the **vaccines** you need is another way you can help stay healthy. A vaccine is a kind of medicine that prevents a person from getting a disease. Thanks to vaccines, you will probably never have the misfortune to get once-common diseases like measles and polio.

Staying Away from Germs   There are still no vaccines for many infectious diseases. There is no mystery about the best way to keep from catching these diseases, though. Just stay away from people who have them!

   You should try not to handle things that belong to sick people. Above all, never put something a sick person has touched in your mouth!

   One of the best ways to keep from picking up germs is to wash your hands with hot water and soap. This kills some germs and keeps them from getting from your hands to your mouth.

Disease, Past and Future

There has always been disease in the world, but people have not always understood much about it. Before the microscope was invented, people didn't know there were such things as germs. They didn't know how germs spread from person to person. They didn't understand how dangerous it was to eat dirty food or drink dirty water. They didn't know why it was so important to keep their bodies clean. They didn't understand what caused disease, how to prevent disease, or how to cure it. Disease was a big mystery.

Today, with all that we know about disease, the mystery is still not solved. People still get sick. Scientists all over the world are trying to solve this mystery. They know that the more we learn about the causes of disease, the more we will know about preventing and curing disease.

Comprehension Check

Think and Discuss

1. How do we know that the mystery of disease has not been completely solved?
2. Look at the map on page 251. In which states did Rocky Mountain spotted fever first appear?
3. What are two ways in which viruses differ from bacteria?
4. What are three things you can do to keep from getting an infectious disease?
5. What are some things you do when you're sick to make yourself feel better?

See your Thinker's Handbook for tips.

● Study Skill: Maps

Communication Workshop

Talk

Do you suppose people long ago got more infectious diseases than people do today? Discuss this question with a panel of your classmates. Try to give facts to back up your opinion.

Speaking/Listening: Panel discussion

Write

Make a list of things we know about disease today that people long ago did not know. Add your list to your classmates'. Help make a Master Copy that combines the facts from everyone's lists.

Writing Fluency: List

There Is One That Has a Head Without an Eye

by Christina Rossetti

There is one that has a head
    without an eye,
  And there's one that has an eye
    without a head:
You may find the answer if you try
    And when all is said,
  Half the answer hangs upon a thread.

Meet the Poet

Christina Rossetti was born in London, England, in 1830. Her life as a child was different from the lives of most children. The youngest child in a family of poets and painters, she was taught at home by her mother. Since her father came from Italy, the family spoke Italian as well as English. Young Christina began writing in two languages before most children write in one.

Rossetti's health was not good, but she was a pretty, playful child. One game she liked was a rhyming game. She and her brothers thought up rhymes and then made up poems using the rhymes in the same order they had thought of them.

Rossetti's first book of poems was printed by her grandfather for their family and friends when she was twelve. Other people first read her poems in a magazine called *The Germ.*

Most of Rossetti's poems are about love, children, nature, faith, and death. Though many of her poems are sad, some are light and happy. She wrote *Sing-Song: A Nursery Rhyme Book* for children. The poems in this book remind some people of Mother Goose rhymes.

When Rossetti was in her forties, she became ill and never really recovered. She stayed at home and had few visitors, but she continued to write poetry until she died in 1894. Almost one hundred years later, people still read and enjoy her poems.

Learning About Word Histories

There's a mystery in the sentence below the illustration. That is the mystery of the words in the sentence. Where did the word *mystery* itself come from? How about *private eye* and *clue?*

Every word has a story, or history, about how it came to be. Words are born, grow, and change. Some- times the history of a word is funny or surprising.

The word *mystery*, for example, came from a Greek word meaning "to have closed eyes and lips." When *mysterie* entered the English language long ago, it had the meaning of something you believed but couldn't prove. Now *mystery* means something you don't understand.

Detectives have been called private eyes ever since the 1860s when Pinkerton, a large detective firm, printed the words "We never sleep" on cards and posters. The words are written over a drawing of an open eye.

A private eye solves a mystery by studying clues.

When the word *clue* was first used in English, it meant "ball of thread." *Clue* may be traced back to a Greek word used for the thread that helped people find their way through a maze. So then, as now, a clue was something that helped people solve a mystery.

Reading Word Histories

Read the histories of the words below.

diagram   The word comes from two Greek words, *dia* which means "through" and *graphein* which means "draw" or "write." A diagram is a drawing marked out by lines to show the important parts of something. *You will see a diagram in the article about the sounds dolphins make.*

signature   The word comes from a Latin word that means "mark" or "seal." A signature is a person's name written by that person. *Write your signature on the letter.*

Tips for Understanding and Enjoying Language
- Words come into English in many ways and from many languages.
- Learning word histories can help you understand and enjoy our language.
- For more tips on figuring out words, see your Word Study Handbook.

Dolphins make several kinds of noises. Scientists have figured out why dolphins make some sounds. Other sounds remain a mystery. The diagram will help you understand one kind of noises dolphins make.

The Sounds of Dolphins
by Scott Lewis

Did You Know?
Dolphins live in the water, but they are not fish. Dolphins are mammals. Female mammals give milk to their young. Horses, chimpanzees, and humans are among the many mammals.

A blindfolded dolphin is swimming in a large tank of water. The dolphin's trainer throws a fish into the tank. Quickly, the dolphin swims straight to the fish and catches and eats it. How could the dolphin find a fish it could not see?

An injured dolphin is alone. As it sinks to the ocean floor, it whistles over and over. In moments, the dolphin is surrounded by other dolphins who push the hurt one to the surface of the water. The injured dolphin breathes deeply. Soon it is strong enough to swim away. Did the injured dolphin's whistles tell the others something? Were the whistles calls for help?

To look for answers to these questions, we must go under the ocean. The ocean is a place we do not understand very well. It is a place filled with mysterious sounds, where ears are more important than eyes.

The Dolphin's Noisy Home

In the ocean, waterfalls rumble and rocks tumble and crash, just as they do on land. Undersea animals make sounds. Shrimp snap their claws, crabs pound on the ocean floor, and fish grunt, squeak, and cackle. The ocean is a noisy place.

Dolphins make sounds too. They make clicking sounds, like the ticking of a clock. They whistle and chirp. They groan, grunt, and make sounds like a creaking door.

To people, the ocean seems quiet. If we put our heads underwater, we cannot hear very much. That is because air gets trapped inside our ears and blocks the sound. To listen to undersea sounds we have to use a hydrophone.

hydrophone (hī′drə fōn), instrument used to hear sounds underwater and to tell where they are coming from.

Sounds That Bounce

The blindfolded dolphin used sounds to find the fish in its tank. The dolphin did this by listening to *echoes*.

An echo is made when a sound bounces off something. Sometimes you can hear echoes in a canyon, a tunnel, or a big empty room with a high ceiling. If you shout "Hello" in one of those places, your "Hello" will come back to you as one or more echoes. Underwater sounds make echoes too.

As they swim, dolphins make clicking sounds. Then they listen for echoes of the clicks. By listening to the echoes, the blindfolded dolphin found the fish in the tank.

Look at the diagram. The dolphin makes a clicking sound. The sound travels through the water toward the fish. When the sound reaches the fish, it bounces off the fish's body and sends an echo back to the dolphin.

Dolphin using echolocation

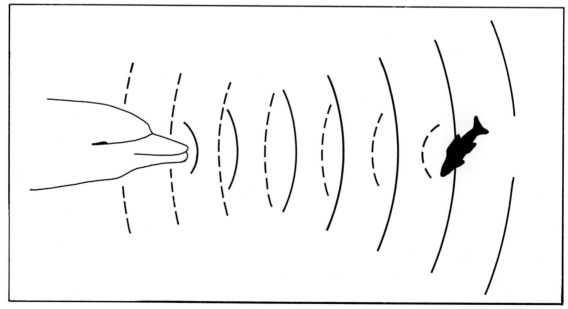

Echolocation is one way of finding something by using sound. Dolphins are very good at using echolocation. They can aim their clicks very well and can hear even the softest echoes.

When a dolphin uses echolocation, it makes many clicks very fast. A dolphin can make hundreds of clicks in a second. By making clicks and listening for the echoes, a dolphin can find out how big something is, what its shape is like, and how far away it is. Using echolocation, dolphins in experiments have found thin wires and tiny marbles. Dolphins can even tell one kind of fish from another.

echolocation
(ek′ ō lō kā ′shən), finding out where something is and what it is like by using echoes.

Did You Know?
Dolphins are not the only animals that use echolocation. Fish, whales, and hippopotamuses use it in water. Bats and some kinds of birds use it in air.

Did You Know?
Echolocation
equipment is used
on ships to find out
how deep the
water is. It is also
used to search for
fish. But the
equipment made
by people does not
work nearly as
well as a dolphin's
echolocation.

Most dolphins have good eyesight, but they still need echolocation. If the water is muddy or if they dive deep in the ocean where it is dark, then they have to use echolocation. Some kinds of dolphins that live in rivers in India and China are almost blind. They use echolocation all the time.

There are many things we still don't know about the dolphin's echolocation. How can dolphins make so many clicks so fast? How can they aim the clicks so well? How can they hear such soft echoes? Though we know how echolocation works, we do not know how dolphins do it so well.

Dolphin Signals

Dolphins often whistle, squeak, and chatter to each other. They use these sounds to make signals. Do you remember the injured dolphin? The whistle the dolphin made was a signal to other dolphins, asking them to come and help. Scientists who study dolphins have learned the meanings of some signals dolphins make.

Every dolphin has a special whistle, or a signal, of its own. That whistle, called a signature whistle, is like a name. Signature whistles sound like birdsongs. A dolphin often makes its signature whistle while it swims. If dolphins are far apart, their signature whistles help them find each other.

When a dolphin is surprised or frightened, it makes a loud crack like the sound of a stick breaking. To a person listening with a hydrophone, it is like hearing a loud thunderclap during a rainstorm. The sound travels far underwater to alert other dolphins.

Dolphins make other signals too. If a group of dolphins is scattered, one of the leaders can call out for all of them to meet together. Mother dolphins signal to their babies to stay close by.

Signals and Language

Almost all animals make signals to warn each other of danger. They make signals to show that they are angry or hungry. They signal to tell other animals to stay away. But most animals make only a few different signals because they can only make a few sounds.

These signals do not give much information. A signal that means "I am hurt" does not tell how the animal got hurt, what is wrong with it, or how badly it is hurt. To give information like this, an animal would have to use some kind of language.

Dolphins make many sounds. Scientists have counted about two thousand different whistles that dolphins can make. Because dolphins make so many sounds, scientists wonder if dolphins give each other more information than signals can give. Do dolphins have a language of their own?

What Do Dolphins Say?

Scientists know that dolphins answer each other. If one dolphin whistles, the dolphins nearby whistle back. To learn more about dolphins answering each other, scientists have done experiments with dolphins and telephones.

Two dolphins named Doris and Dash were in an experiment in 1965. Scientists who worked for the Navy put Doris in one tank and Dash in another. Then underwater telephones were set up so Doris and Dash could hear one another.

At first, Doris whistled and chattered while Dash listened. Then Dash made sounds while Doris was quiet. The dolphins did not make sounds at the same time.

Were Doris and Dash talking to each other as two people talking on a telephone do? Many of the dolphins' whistles seemed to be signature whistles. But what about the other sounds Doris and Dash made? Were they signals? Were they language? Or were they nonsense?

In 1962, some scientists thought they might have heard dolphins talking to each other in the ocean. The scientists were in a boat near the shore. As part of an experiment, they had put a row of metal poles under water. Suddenly, they saw five dolphins swimming toward the row of poles. Using hydrophones, the scientists could hear the clicking of the dolphins' echolocation.

When the dolphins were about five hundred yards away from the poles, they stopped swimming. A few minutes later, one dolphin swam up close to the poles. It swam from one end of the row to the other, making clicks the whole time. Then the dolphin swam back to the others. When it reached them, the dolphins whistled and chattered to each other.

Then a second dolphin swam up to the poles and explored them using its echolocation. When it returned to the group, the whistling and chattering started again. A third dolphin did the same thing.

Finally, all five dolphins swam up to the row of poles together. They swam between the poles and through to the other side.

To the scientists, it seemed that the dolphins were talking to each other. But just as in the experiment with Doris and Dash, no one knows what the dolphins' whistling and chattering meant.

Teaching Dolphins to Talk

Several groups of scientists are trying a different kind of experiment with dolphins. They are trying to teach dolphins a simple language. They want to find out if dolphins can learn a language like the one we use.

One of the groups of scientists is working in Hawaii. Using a computer and other equipment, the scientists make whistles that sound like dolphin whistles. Each whistle stands for a different word. So far, the dolphins have learned the meanings of about twenty-five whistles.

One of the dolphins can repeat a few of the whistles the scientists make. If someone throws a ball into the tank, the dolphin makes the whistle that means "ball."

The scientists also put whistles together to make short sentences. Then they see if the dolphins understand the sentences. If a scientist makes four whistles that mean "ball fetch bottom hoop," the dolphin will take the ball and put it in a hoop at the bottom of the tank. A scientist might make whistles that say "ball question." That means "Is there a ball in the tank?" To answer the question, the dolphin presses one lever for yes or another lever for no. Most of the time, the dolphins push the correct lever.

Do these experiments show that dolphins can learn to understand a language like ours? Some scientists say yes, but others say no. It is still too soon to know for sure. The main thing the experiments have shown so far is that dolphins are very smart animals.

Still a Mystery

As much as we have learned about dolphins and the sounds they make, many questions still remain. What do all those undersea whistles, chirps, and groans mean? Do dolphins have a language of their own? Will we be able to talk to dolphins someday?

To solve the mystery of the sounds of the dolphin, we will have to learn much more about the dolphins and their ocean home. Maybe we will never answer all the questions we have about dolphins. Some of the sounds dolphins make may always be a mystery to us.

Comprehension Check

Think and Discuss

1. Why do dolphins make clicking sounds?
• 2. Look at the diagram on page 264. What bounces back to the dolphin from the fish?
3. Which sounds that dolphins make are signals?
4. How do language experiments show that dolphins are smart?
5. Do you think dolphins have their own language? Why or why not?

● Study Skill: Diagrams

Communication Workshop

Talk

Interview classmates or members of your family. Then ask what questions they would like to ask a dolphin. What questions might a dolphin ask them?

Speaking/Listening: Interviewing

Write

Write three questions *you* would like to ask a dolphin. Then write several questions you think the dolphin would like to ask you. Exchange questions with a friend. Make up answers for one another.

Writing Fluency: Questions

Ask Yourself Questions

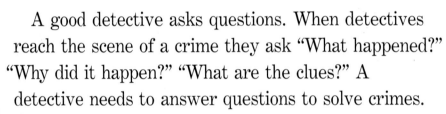

A good detective asks questions. When detectives reach the scene of a crime they ask "What happened?" "Why did it happen?" "What are the clues?" A detective needs to answer questions to solve crimes.

You need to ask questions to understand what you read, just as a detective does to solve a crime. Asking questions and finding the answers as you read help you figure out what's important in a selection. Here are some questions you can ask before you read.

- What is the selection about?
- What kinds of things will the author tell you about the subject?
- What kind of selection will this be, entertaining, informative, or persuasive?

When you finish reading, think again about your questions. Did you find the answers you were looking for? Did you think of any new questions? You will understand and remember a selection better if you ask questions.

How does Captain Gadwall predict the future? The details in the story can help you figure out the answer before Miss Mallard does.

Rickshaw to Horror

by Robert Quackenbush

All of Hong Kong was celebrating the Dragon Boat Festival. Boat-racing teams had come from all over the world. On one street, a Dragon Dance went weaving back and forth through the crowd. Suddenly, a rickshaw raced ahead of the dragon.

"Lee Long Duck!" cried Miss Mallard, the world-famous ducktective. "Please slow down! You're going much too fast! How can I see the sights of Hong Kong at this speed?"

"Sorry," said Lee Long Duck.

Lee Long Duck quickly turned a corner onto a quieter street. At the same moment, someone stepped off the sidewalk and was knocked down by the rickshaw.

"Horrors!" cried Miss Mallard. "We hit someone!"

Lee Long Duck stopped the rickshaw. Miss Mallard jumped out and looked under it as a police officer came running over.

"Are you all right under there?" called Miss Mallard. "I'm Margery Mallard. I've seen you before. We're staying at the same hotel. I'm terribly sorry about this."

"Marshall Gadwall, retired navy captain, here," quacked a weak voice. "I'm fine. Just a bit dizzy from hitting my head."

Gadwall crawled out from under the rickshaw. He looked dazed.

"Perhaps you should see a doctor," said the police officer.

"No, no," said Gadwall. "I am quite all right. Besides, this is Sunday and it is nearly ten o'clock. I must be off to an important meeting."

"But today is Saturday," said Miss Mallard.

"No, Sunday," said Gadwall. "Don't you remember? At this same hour yesterday—Saturday—someone raised a storm warning flag at the ferry. All the ferries stopped running and everyone rushed for shelter."

The police officer said, "I'll prove to you that today is Saturday."

He called someone on his walkie-talkie. When he finished, he looked at Gadwall.

"Great Dragons!" he said. "Someone *did* raise a fake warning flag at the ferry building just now. The crowd is in a panic and the police are trying to sort things out. But how could you predict it? It must be a coincidence. You had better go to your hotel now. I'm Officer Pintail, if you should need me again."

"I'll take Captain Gadwall to the hotel," said Miss Mallard. "It's just around the corner."

At the hotel, Gadwall decided to have some tea. He asked Miss Mallard to join him.

"I never could turn down a cup of tea," said Miss Mallard.

"Good!" said Gadwall. "I'll meet you in the restaurant. I must send my servant, Harold, on an errand. My wife, Melissa, is shopping and should return soon. I'd like you two to meet."

Miss Mallard went into the restaurant. At a table by the window, she sat down facing the lobby. While she was waiting, she took a travel guidebook from

her knitting bag and began to read. The book said that a million-dollar jade necklace was on display at the Duckworth Museum.

"I'd like to see that," she thought.

Miss Mallard looked up and saw Gadwall talking to Harold, who was wearing a gray jacket. Then Harold left, and Mrs. Gadwall came into the hotel. Gadwall brought his wife into the restaurant.

"I'm pleased to meet you," said Melissa Gadwall. "Are you here for the Dragon Boat Festival?"

"Yes," said Miss Mallard. "And you?"

"I prefer shopping," said Melissa Gadwall. "Especially for jade."

Marshall Gadwall cleared his throat and changed the subject. He told his wife about the accident.

"And the strangest thing, dear!" Gadwall said. "When I was hit on the head, I could predict things."

"Like what?" asked his wife.

Suddenly, Gadwall turned very silent. He looked at his watch. Then he looked at Miss Mallard.

"What's wrong?" asked Miss Mallard.

"In exactly five minutes," said Gadwall, "it will be twelve o'clock. That's when someone will cut the ropes of the famous Peeking Duck Floating Restaurant and set it to drift in the harbor."

Miss Mallard gasped and got up from the table.

"What is this about?" cried Melissa Gadwall.

"It is another of your husband's predictions!" said Miss Mallard. "Wait here. I'll notify the police!"

Miss Mallard ran outside. She saw Lee Long Duck and waved to him. He rushed over with his rickshaw and Miss Mallard climbed in.

"Take me to Officer Pintail!" said Miss Mallard. "And forget what I said before. This time you can hurry!"

They found Officer Pintail on a side street. Miss Mallard told him about the new prediction.

"I'll check it out," said Officer Pintail. "The restaurant is only a few blocks away."

They all rushed to the waterfront. When they got there, the Peeking Duck Floating Restaurant had been cut loose from its ropes. It was drifting out to sea. Everyone on board was quacking loudly to be saved. Officer Pintail called for help on his walkie-talkie.

In a flash, firetrucks and police cars came racing to the waterfront. At the same time, out in the harbor, boats were at work. They pushed the restaurant back to shore.

When the floating restaurant was safe, Officer Pintail filled out a report. The restaurant manager said that he did not know who cut the ropes. He asked who had sounded the alarm.

"I did," said Miss Mallard.

"I am very grateful to you," said the manager. "Please be our guest for dinner any time."

"In fact," said Miss Mallard, "someone at my hotel, Marshall Gadwall, warned me that you were in danger."

"Please invite him to dinner, too," said the manager.

Miss Mallard said that she would. Then she went looking for Lee Long Duck. On the way, she saw a gray thread hanging from one of the cut ropes of the floating restaurant.

"Hmmmm," she said.

She looked at the thread with her magnifying glass. Then she put it between the pages of her travel guide and put the book back in her knitting bag. After that, she found Lee Long Duck and rode away in his rickshaw.

When Miss Mallard at last returned to the hotel, she found Gadwall alone in the restaurant. He said that Mrs. Gadwall had gone shopping again. Miss

Mallard told him how his second prediction had come true. She also told him about the manager's dinner invitation.

"That was nice of him," said Gadwall. "But I won't be able to go. Floating restaurants make me seasick."

Just then, Officer Pintail arrived. He needed some information for his report on the restaurant. He asked Gadwall how he was able to predict bad events.

"I have no idea," said Gadwall. "Ever since the rickshaw accident, pictures just seem to pop into my head."

Suddenly he stopped talking and looked at his watch. "What is it?" asked Miss Mallard.

Gadwall answered, "In five minutes, it will be exactly three o'clock. That's when someone will let the air out of the tires of all the tour buses at the Victoria Market. There will be a major traffic jam."

Officer Pintail was alarmed.

"Wait here!" he said to Gadwall as he ran from the hotel.

Miss Mallard ran, too. She hired Lee Long Duck to take her to the market. When she got there, she saw all the flat tires and the major traffic jam that Gadwall had described. There were ducks everywhere, nearly quacking their heads off. And just as before, the police could not find out who had done it.

It was several hours before the tires were fixed and the police unsnarled the traffic. All the while, Miss Mallard kept looking for clues. But she found nothing. Finally, she had Lee Long Duck take her back to the hotel. But when she got there, she saw many reporters crowding around the front door.

"Horrors!" said Miss Mallard. "The news is out about Gadwall's predictions."

Miss Mallard squeezed past the reporters and went into the hotel. She saw Officer Pintail and the police chief questioning Gadwall in the restaurant.

"I know what I know," Gadwall was saying. "Tomorrow morning at exactly ten o'clock, during the boat races, some of the boats will be destroyed. A big fight will break out and the Dragon Boat Festival will end in disaster."

"We must prevent that from happening," said Officer Pintail.

"I'll send a large police force to the races in the morning," said the chief.

Miss Mallard was puzzled. Why did all of Gadwall's predictions involve the police? She excused herself and went to her room. It had been a very tiring day, and she needed to be alone so she could think.

She ordered supper in her room. All evening she went over the events of the day. But at bedtime she was still as puzzled as ever.

Miss Mallard thought about her only clue, the gray thread, which she had placed in her travel book. She opened the guidebook. The thread was still there. She closed the book again and stared at it. Then she put it away and went to sleep.

When Miss Mallard woke up the next morning, it was already nine o'clock. And Gadwall's prediction was set for ten!

Miss Mallard leaped out of bed. Suddenly everything was clear to her! She grabbed her knitting bag. She reached inside and gave her travel guide a pat. Then she dug through her clipping file for a news story she needed.

"Horrors!" she said when she found it.

Quickly, she got dressed and ran to the front desk. She asked where she could find the Gadwalls.

"Sorry," said the clerk. "They checked out this morning."

"I thought so!" said Miss Mallard.

She rushed outside.

"Quick!" she cried to Lee Long Duck. "Take me to Officer Pintail."

When they found Officer Pintail, Miss Mallard said, "It's about the Gadwalls! They left the hotel! Right at this moment I believe that they are stealing the million-dollar jade necklace that is on display at the Duckworth Museum! The accident and predictions were faked! The Gadwalls planned to keep the police busy so the museum would be less protected against robbery!"

"Great Dragons!" said Officer Pintail. "I'll send a police car to the museum right away!"

Lee Long Duck sped with Miss Mallard to the museum. Officer Pintail and the other police were already there. They were crowded around the museum's side door.

Miss Mallard went over. She saw Marshall Gadwall, Melissa Gadwall, and Harold, all in handcuffs.

"Well, you were right, Miss Mallard," said Officer Pintail. "We caught them in the act, just as they were coming out the door with the necklace."

"How did you know we would be here?" grumbled Marshall Gadwall.

"Thanks to my guidebook," said Miss Mallard. "I saw a picture of the jade necklace in it, and I remembered that your wife said she was 'shopping' for jade. I also remembered that you said you were a retired navy captain. Since when do navy captains get seasick on floating restaurants? Then all it took was a look in my clipping file to find out who you really are—'Slippery' Gadwall, the well-known thief and swindler."

Miss Mallard paused and reached into her knitting bag. She pulled out the gray thread.

"Here is a thread that I found at the floating restaurant," said Miss Mallard. "As you can see, it matches Harold's jacket. Not only that, you said that your wife had gone shopping yesterday morning. Yet she returned to the hotel empty-handed. I believe that you sent your wife and Harold out to make the events that you 'predicted' happen. You followed me to fake the rickshaw accident, knowing that I would call for the police. It was all a scheme to fool the police, so the museum would be less protected while you robbed it."

"Take them away," said Officer Pintail. "I'll tell the chief that there will be no trouble at the Dragon Boat Races."

Then Officer Pintail turned to Miss Mallard and said, "Good job!"

"Well, I'm glad we saved the necklace," said Miss Mallard. "The Gadwalls had me fooled for a while."

Lee Long Duck said, "How about seeing the sights of Hong Kong now—very slowly?"

"Why, Lee Long!" said Miss Mallard. "What a good idea!"

Comprehension Check

Think and Discuss

1. How does Captain Gadwall make it seem as though he can predict the future?
- 2. What happens first to make Miss Mallard think the Gadwalls may be up to no good?
- 3. What does Miss Mallard find that proves she is right to suspect the Gadwalls?
4. Does Miss Mallard have the qualities a good detective needs? Why or why not?
5. What mystery would you like Miss Mallard to help you solve?

- Comprehension: Details

Communication Workshop

Talk

Get together with a group of classmates and pretend you are mystery writers. Discuss what good mystery stories need. Do you think *Rickshaw to Horror* is a good mystery? Then give one another the names of some other good mystery stories you have read.

Speaking/Listening: Cooperative learning

Write

Think of another mystery for Miss Mallard to solve. Write a paragraph describing the mystery. Read it aloud to your "Mystery Writers Group."

Writing Fluency: Paragraph

LOOKING BACK

Thinking and Writing About the Section

In this section you've read about mysteries. You can write a persuasive paragraph to convince your class about why a mystery is important. First copy this chart and fill it in.

See your Thinker's Handbook for tips.

Selection	Mystery to Solve	Why It's Important
"The Mystery of Disease"	how to stop disease	

Writing

Choose one of the mysteries you listed above and write a persuasive paragraph about why it is important. State your opinion in a topic sentence. Then give at least two reasons to back it up. See your Writer's Handbook for more help.

Revising

Read your first draft to a partner. Are your reasons strong? Make changes, proofread, and write a final copy.

Presenting

Read your persuasive paragraph to your class. Did you convince them?

6

Journeys

What does the word *journey* mean to you? Is it a trip far away? A trip to a distant land is a journey. But a journey can be close to home. It can begin when you curl up in a comfortable chair to think and dream. That kind of journey is one you take in your mind. A journey is important when it helps you learn about the world and about yourself.

In this Section you'll read about three journeys. The characters learn and grow because of their journeys. Come join them.

Finding Goal and Outcome

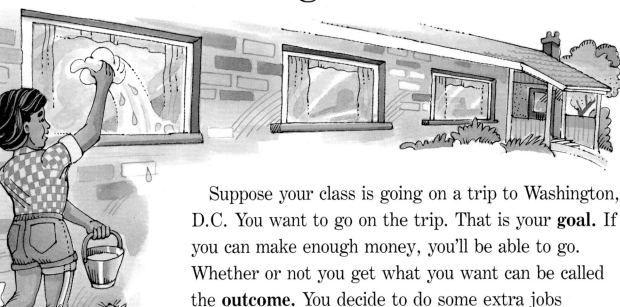

Suppose your class is going on a trip to Washington, D.C. You want to go on the trip. That is your **goal.** If you can make enough money, you'll be able to go. Whether or not you get what you want can be called the **outcome.** You decide to do some extra jobs around the house to make money. This is how you will try to reach your goal.

Characters in stories have goals too. The characters may do many things to reach their goals. Sometimes characters get what they want and other times they don't. The outcome of a story shows whether the characters get what they want.

Knowing what the character's goal is can help you understand why the character does certain things to reach the goal.

As you read the paragraph on the next page, find out what Tom's goal is and the outcome of the story.

Tom had always wanted to swim across the lake. This was his fourth try. He had failed to make the two-mile swim three times before. Tom had spent a lot of time practicing swimming long distances.

As Tom swam, he knew this time would be different. He felt stronger and in better shape. Suddenly Tom could hear cheers. He looked up and saw his friends waiting for him on land. He had done it—a two-mile swim!

Answer the following questions.

1. What was Tom's goal?

To answer this question, look back at the first paragraph. The first sentence says that Tom wanted to swim across the lake.

2. What did he do to reach his goal? Look back at the fourth sentence in the first paragraph.

3. What was the outcome of the story? Look at the last sentence in the second paragraph.

Practicing Goal and Outcome

As you read the following story, think about Janet's goal and the outcome of the story.

I cried the day my father came home and said, "Janet, I have a new job in a new city." I did not want to move away from my friends. I made up my mind that I was *not* moving to a new city. I did everything I could to try to change my father's mind. I cooked his favorite dinner and even cleaned my bedroom. Nothing helped. We moved, but you know what? I'm beginning to think I might learn to like it here.

1. What was Janet's goal?
2. What did Janet do to try to reach her goal?
3. What was the outcome of the story?

Tips for Reading on Your Own

- Find the characters' goals, or what they want.
- Look for the ways characters reach their goals.
- Decide the outcome, or whether the characters reach their goals.

Evan's travels around his neighborhood make him want one thing more than anything else in the world. Read to find out Evan's goal and the outcome of the story.

Evan's Corner

by Elizabeth Starr Hill

Evan walked home from school slowly. He stopped in front of a pet shop. In the window, a canary sang to him from its golden cage. Canary bird has its own cage, Evan thought. I want a place of my own.

He walked on. A bright pink flower on a window sill caught his eye. Flower has its own pot, he thought. Wish *I* had a place of my own.

He kept going until he reached the big crossing. He waited by the newsstand for the light to change.

Paper man has his own stand, he thought. And I, me, myself—*I* need a place of my own.

He crossed the noisy, busy street and turned into the building where he lived. He trudged up four flights of steep stairs to the two rooms that he and his family shared.

Soon his three sisters and his two brothers would come home. Then his mother and then his father.

Mighty lot of family, Evan thought. And no place to call just *mine.*

Evan wore a door key on a string around his neck so he could unlock the door. Usually he was the first one home. But today the door flew open before he touched it.

"Surprise!" His mother stood laughing in the doorway. "Mrs. Thompson said I could leave early. I beat you home, Evan!" Mrs. Thompson was the lady his mother cleaned for.

Evan gave his mother a big hug. He liked it when she got home ahead of him. Now they could have a private talk before his brothers and sisters came in.

"Mama, you know what I've been wishing for *hard?*" Evan burst out.

"Tell me." His mother smiled.

Evan told her the canary bird had a cage. He told her the flower had a pot. He told her the paper man had a newsstand. He ended, "And I want a place of my own."

His mother thought and thought. At first it seemed she might not find a way.

But then her face lighted up.

"Why, of course!" she said. "It will work out just right. There are eight of us. That means each one of us can have a corner!"

Evan jumped to his feet and clapped his hands. "Can I choose mine?"

"Yes." She nodded. "Go ahead. You have first choice, Evan."

Evan ran to every corner of the rooms. One corner had a pretty edge of rug. Some had nothing much. One had an interesting crack in the wall.

But the one Evan liked best, the one he wanted for his own, had a nice small window and a bit of polished floor.

"This is mine," Evan said happily. "This is my corner."

That night he paid no attention to the rest of the family. He sat alone and content on the floor, in his corner.

His little brother Adam asked him, "Why you want a corner of your own, Evan?"

Evan thought for a minute. "I want a chance to be lonely."

Adam tiptoed away and left him.

When supper was ready, Evan's father came to Evan's corner.

"Stew's on the table," he told him. "You want to eat with us, Evan?"

"Please, Pa," Evan asked, "if I bring my plate here, can I eat by myself?"

"Why, sure," his father said.

So Evan fetched his plate of stew and sat down on the floor again.

His family ate at the table in the next room. From his corner, Evan could see them. He heard them talking and laughing.

At dessert time, he joined them.

"Why, Evan!" His father smiled. "I thought you wanted to eat by yourself."

Evan smiled back at him. "I was lonely," he said.

After supper, there were jobs to do. Evan helped clear the table. He brushed his teeth. He studied for school.

When his work was done, he sat in his corner again. He looked out the window.

Adam came behind Evan and said softly, "Are you being lonely now?"

"No," Evan answered.

"What *are* you doing then?"

"I'm wasting time," Evan told him. "In my own way. In my own corner."

Adam asked, "Can I ever come into your corner, Evan?"

"Why don't you choose a corner of your own?" Evan said.

So Adam did. He chose the corner across the room from Evan's. He sat in it. He called, "What shall I do in my corner, Evan?"

"Whatever you like."

But Adam didn't know what to do. After a minute, he left his corner. He played horse with his big sister Lucy. He sat on her back and held on to her pigtails. "Gid-yup, Lucy-horse!" he shouted. They galloped round and round the room.

Next morning, as soon as he woke up, Evan ran to his corner. His bit of polished floor shone as brightly as ever. His window was still fun to look through.

But Evan felt that his corner needed something more.

What could it be?

He stared at the bare walls. I know! he thought suddenly. I need me a picture! And I'll make it myself!

In school that morning, Evan painted a picture of the sea. He drew big waves and a green boat.

He told his teacher, "I'm going to hang this picture in my own corner!"

"That will be lovely, Evan," his teacher said.

Evan could hardly wait to get home after school. He taped the picture to the wall beside the window in his corner. He stepped back to look at it.

The green boat seemed to bob on the blue waves. It bobbed too much. Evan realized the picture was crooked.

He straightened it. Now it looked just right.

Adam came home with their biggest sister, Gloria. She always picked Adam up at the day-care center on her way home from school.

Adam's eyes shone as he saw the picture. "That's mighty pretty, Evan!" he said. "Do you think I could draw a picture for my corner?"

"Sure you could."

Adam ran off. But he could not find any paper. He had no crayons. Lucy had crayons, but she was busy with homework now. He did not dare speak to her.

He returned to Evan.

Evan sat in his corner with his back to the room. He looked up at his picture.

Adam asked softly, "Are you being lonely, Evan?"

"No."

"Are you wasting your own time in your own way?"

"No," Evan told him.

"Well, then, what are you doing?"

"Enjoying peace and quiet," Evan said.

Adam tiptoed off.

That night, Evan did not sleep well. He lay awake in bed, thinking about his corner. It had a nice floor and a nice window and a nice picture. But was that enough?

No, he decided finally. I need something more. But what?

He remembered the pink flower in its pot. He thought: That's it! I need a plant of my own, in my own corner.

On Saturday, Evan went to the playground. He took his toothbrush glass and a spoon.

The paving of the playground was cracked. Grass and weeds grew up through the broken concrete.

Evan found a weed that had big, lacy flowers on it. He dug it up with his spoon. He planted it in his toothbrush glass.

Then he took it home and put it on the window sill, in his own corner.

Adam came over to see what was going on. "What you doing, Evan?" he asked.

"Watching my plant grow," Evan told him.

"Maybe I'll have a plant, too, someday," Adam said softly.

Evan didn't answer. Something was bothering him.

Even now, his corner seemed not quite perfect. And he didn't know why.

I got me no furniture, he realized at last. Why didn't I think of that before?

Evan skipped off to the grocery store. He asked Mr. Meehan for two old orange crates.

"What do you want them for?" Mr. Meehan asked.

"Going to make me some furniture," Evan said proudly. "To put in a place of my own."

Mr. Meehan let him have the crates.

In his corner, Evan stood one of the crates up on end. Now it was like a high desk. He turned the other crate upside down to make a bench. He sat on the bench.

Surely he had all anyone could wish for.

And yet . . .

How come I feel like something's still missing? Evan wondered.

He puzzled and puzzled it over. Suddenly he remembered the canary bird in its cage.

A great idea struck him: I know! I need a pet to take care of. A pet of my own, in my own corner. And he ran out to the pet shop.

He looked at the canary bird in the window. Well, canary bird, he thought, you sing fine. But you're not the pet for me.

He walked into the store. A goldfish swam over to the edge of its bowl and stared at him.

"Afternoon, Mister Fish," Evan said politely. But he thought: No sir. That's not the pet for me.

He moved on to the turtle tank. A sign above it read: "Bargain! Special! Turtle with bowl, only 50¢!" Beside the tank, a neat row of empty little bowls waited.

Evan peered into the tank. Ten or twelve lively baby green turtles swam and scrambled all over each other. One climbed up on a rock in the middle

308

of the water. It looked at Evan. He felt like laughing. It must have been the funniest turtle in the world!

That baby turtle had the *scrawniest* neck. Its feet were big and ugly. Its eyes were merry and black. If a turtle could smile, that turtle was smiling.

It took a dive off the rock. Clumsy turtle! It landed upside down in the shallow water! Its legs waved wildly in the air.

Evan turned it over carefully. The turtle winked at him as though it knew a secret. It looked as cheerful as ever.

"Yes sir, yes sir!" Evan told that funny little turtle joyfully. "*You're* the pet for me!"

Evan's heart beat hard and fast. He asked the pet-shop man, "Please, mister, do you have a job a boy can do? I'd mighty much like to earn enough to buy a turtle!"

"Sorry, son, I don't need help. Try next door," the pet-shop man suggested.

Evan went next door to the Chinese bakery and asked for work. "Ah, no," Mr. Fong told him gently. "My sons help me. Try across the street."

Evan crossed the street. He marched from store to store, asking for work. He had no luck.

Maybe some lady would pay me to carry her packages, Evan thought.

He turned in at the supermarket. He stood by the check-out counter. A lady came through. Evan asked, "Carry your bags, lady?"

She did not answer. She walked on by.

Evan waited for the next lady. This time he smiled extra politely and spoke a little louder. "Excuse me, but those bags look mighty heavy. Carry them for you?"

"Why, yes." She put them in his arms. "That would be a big help."

Evan carried the groceries up the block to where she lived. The lady thanked him. She gave him a dime. A dime! He had a dime! Now all he needed was four more!

Evan raced back to the supermarket. He stood by the check-out. He waited. He smiled. He spoke politely.

Lots of ladies went past. But none of them wanted him to carry her bags.

Just as Evan began to fear that he would never make another cent, a young girl said, "Oh, good! I hate lugging bundles!"

She, too, gave Evan a dime.

Only three more to go, he thought happily.

On Sunday the supermarket was closed. But Evan went there right after school on Monday.

He made one more dime, then another. He had forty cents!

Listen, you turtle! he thought. You're almost mine!

But the next day, he fooled around for a while after school. When he finally got to the supermarket, a bigger boy was there ahead of him.

Evan's heart sank. He had supposed it would be so easy to earn only one dime! He hung around all afternoon, hoping. But the other boy got the jobs. And Evan still had only forty cents.

Next day he rushed from school to the supermarket as fast as his legs would go. Panting, he ran right to the check-out counter. The other boy was not there!

Hurray! Evan thought. Bet this is my lucky day!

At first things were slow. Then, toward closing time, a marvelous moment came. A white-haired lady spoke to him: "Sonny, do you think you could help me with these heavy groceries?"

Evan said eagerly, "Yes ma'am!"

Her bag was still on the counter. It was a huge one, filled clear up to the top. Somehow Evan got his arms around it and hoisted it off the counter. "Where to, lady?" he gasped.

"Why," she said sweetly, "I live just next door." She added, "Three flights up."

Evan staggered out of the store with the bag. He followed the lady next door without much trouble. But he thought he never would get up those stairs. Yet at last he made it. He eased the bag down on the lady's kitchen table.

"Thank you," she said. And she gave him the dime—the wonderful dime—the shining dime that made five!

Evan ran to the pet shop at top speed. He poured the dimes on the counter and said proudly, "I earned some money, mister! I'd like to buy me a turtle!"

The pet-shop man counted the dimes. "All right, son. Choose one," he said.

Evan looked into the tank. His eyes passed from one shining green shell to another.

Suddenly he saw a scrawny neck stretch up from the water. A turtle rose, climbed the rock—and fell off upside down, on his back.

"This one!" Evan picked the turtle up. "This one is mine!"

Evan carried the turtle home in a small bowl. He set it on top of the upturned orange crate.

Adam was already home from the day-care center. He asked excitedly, "What you got now, Evan?"

"My own pet," Evan boasted. "To take care of, in my own corner."

Adam looked at the turtle. It winked at him cheerfully.

Adam wanted to see it closer. But he knew he wasn't allowed in Evan's corner.

"Evan, do you think I could ever have a pet of my own?" Adam asked.

"Sure. When you're much, much older."

Adam wandered sadly away.

Now Evan had many things.

He had a place of his own. He could be lonely there. He could waste time if he liked. He could enjoy peace and quiet.

He had a fine picture to look at.

He had a bench of his own to sit on, by his own window. His plant thrived and grew tall.

Best of all, he had a pet to love and take care of.

Evan spent most of his spare time in his corner. But—it was strange. He just wasn't happy.

I must need something more, Evan thought. But what?

He asked his sisters. They didn't know.

He asked his brothers. They didn't know.

His father wasn't home yet. When his mother came home, Evan said, "Mama, I'm not happy in my corner. What do I need now?"

His mother put her head on one side. Together she and Evan stood off from the corner and looked at it.

Sunlight poured through the window and gleamed on the floor.

The lacy white flower stirred in a breeze.

The turtle seemed to grin through the glass of its bowl.

The painted boat rode a painted wave.

Evan's corner was beautiful. They both saw that.

"Evan," his mother said finally. "Maybe what you need is to leave your corner for a while."

"Why?" Evan asked.

"Well," she said slowly, "just fixing up your own corner isn't enough." She smiled into his eyes. "Maybe you need to step out now, and help somebody else."

She left him. He sat alone on his bench, thinking it over.

Adam came in. "Are you enjoying peace and quiet, Evan?" he asked.

"No," Evan said.

"What are you doing, then?"

Evan said slowly, "I'm planning to borrow Lucy's crayons."

"Why?"

"To help you draw a picture if you want to. I'm planning to help you fix up your corner so it's just the way you want it. I'm going to help you make it the best—the nicest—the very most wonderful corner in the whole world!"

Joy spread over Adam's face—and over Evan's.

They ran across the room together to work on Adam's corner.

Comprehension Check

Think and Discuss

- **1.** What is Evan's goal in the story?
- **2.** Do you think Evan reaches his goal? Why or why not?
- **3.** What does Evan do to fix up his corner?
- **4.** Why isn't Evan happy with his corner after it is fixed up?
- **5.** What lesson does Evan learn from his mother?

See your Thinker's Handbook for tips.

- Literary Skill: Goal and outcome

Communication Workshop

Talk

If you had a corner of your own to fix up, what would you put in it? Would you pick a pet and a plant like Evan did? Think of other things that would make a corner your own special place. Share your ideas with a member of your family.

Speaking/Listening: Discussion

Write

Write a paragraph describing your corner and all the things you would put into it. Read it aloud to someone in your family. Perhaps you could create part of your corner at home.

Writing Fluency: Paragraph

The Land of Nod

by Robert Louis Stevenson

From breakfast on through all the day
At home among my friends I stay,
But every night I go abroad
Afar into the land of Nod.

All by myself I have to go,
With none to tell me what to do—
All alone beside the streams
And up the mountain-sides of dreams.

The strangest things are there for me,
Both things to eat and things to see,
And many frightening sights abroad
Till morning in the land of Nod.

Try as I like to find the way,
I never can get back by day,
Nor can remember plain and clear
The curious music that I hear.

Davy is going on his first trail drive.
Can you predict some of the events
that will happen on the long ride?

Old Blue

by Sibyl Hancock

"Wake up, boy!" Davy opened his eyes. Cookie was
standing over him.

"I'll be right there," Davy said. He pushed his blanket
aside and folded it to make a bedroll. The cowboys
sleeping around the campfire would soon wake up
hungry for breakfast. And the cowboys riding in from
watching the cattle all night would be even hungrier.

A big longhorn steer, with a hide so black it nearly looked blue, lumbered up to Davy and nudged his hand. "Old Blue," Davy said softly. "Are you hungry too?"

Old Blue grunted and shook his horns. Davy laughed. "You think you're better than all those other longhorns. Who ever heard of a big old steer sleeping around the campfire with the cowboys!"

He patted Old Blue's shiny forehead. "You're the smartest old steer I ever saw. Not many ranchers own a steer who can lead all the rest of the cattle on a trail drive."

Davy hurried over to the chuck wagon to help Cookie. He was frying bacon in a black skillet over the fire. "Pa said I can ride today!" Davy exclaimed.

"Huh! Guess you'll feel like a real big shot!" Cookie said. Davy smiled. He would be riding up front with the cowboys who guided the longhorn cattle over the trail. And if Pa said it was okay for him to ride, then it was. Pa was the trail boss.

"You're a lucky boy. Not many young fellows get a chance to go on a trail ride," Cookie told him.

"If Ma hadn't gone to take care of Aunt Clara's new baby, I could never have come," Davy said.

"You can learn plenty on the trail," Cookie said. "But right now there's plenty to do here. Let's get to work!" He handed Davy some tin plates to set out.

"Come and get it!" Cookie yelled. While the cowboys crowded around the chuck wagon, Davy finished his breakfast.

He took a handful of food scraps to Old Blue. The big steer was still eating biscuits and bacon crumbs when Pa brought a horse for Davy to ride.

"Let's get moving," Pa said. "You watch what you're doing up at the front with Old Blue."

"Yes, sir," Davy said.

"Feeling a little shaky?" Pa asked.

Davy nodded.

"I felt the same way on my first trail drive," Pa said. "You'll be fine."

Davy put on his hat. He climbed onto his horse and followed Old Blue up to the head of the herd. One of the cowboys gave the old Texas call, "Ho, cattle, ho, ho, ho, ho!" Soon the steers were strung into a line a mile long with Old Blue leading.

There were over a thousand of them. Davy watched Old Blue walk steadily to the north. No one understood how Old Blue knew directions so well. Sometimes Old Blue walked too fast, and the lead cowboys, or point men, had to slow him down.

What will the weather probably be like during the next two months?

"I don't like the looks of the sky," one of the cowboys said. "It could be a norther." Davy shivered. A norther might bring icy weather, and they had a long way to go.

They had left the Goodnight Ranch in Palo Duro Canyon, Texas, a week ago. It would take two months to bring the herd into Dodge City, Kansas. There the longhorns would be shipped on railroad cars to Chicago.

Davy guided his horse past tumbleweeds rolling slowly in the breeze. Sand crunched under hooves and rose in little gold clouds. Cattle often tried to stop and eat dry clumps of grass. And when they wandered into low mesquite trees, the cowboys had to drive them back to the herd.

Davy looked at the big steer. "Old Blue, you've got your work cut out for you. Here comes the river. We have to get across before the wind changes." The water was icy, but Old Blue plunged right into it. Cattle and cowboys followed.

"Ho, cattle, ho, ho, ho, ho!" Davy yelled. The cold water splashed onto his face. His horse stumbled, and Davy held on tightly. "Keep going," he said. "Don't fall!" His horse began to swim. It seemed like a long time before they reached the other side of the river.

As the cattle came out of the chilly water, they started running to get warm. A thousand longhorns pounded the dusty ground. "Let them run!" Pa shouted. Old Blue would slow them down soon.

By late afternoon the sky grew dark. A streak of lightning flashed. Thunder boomed. There was another sound, too.

Horns rattled together, and hooves pounded the dirt. "Stampede!" Pa cried. "Get out of the way, Davy!" he yelled.

Davy rode his horse away from the frightened steers. He watched the cowboys guide Old Blue around in a circle. The cattle followed. Soon most of the herd were running in a big circle. That was called milling. It was the only way to stop a stampede.

• Do you think Old Blue will be able to help the cowboys stop the stampede? Why or why not?

"Whoa, boy!" Davy cried, trying to calm his horse. The air was full of electricity. Davy could see sparks dancing along the brim of his hat and on the tips of his horse's ears. Pa had called it foxfire. It even sparked from horn tip to horn tip over the milling cattle. As soon as the herd had settled down, Davy rode back to camp.

Cookie was at the chuck wagon building a fire. "Get your slicker on," Cookie said. "It's going to be a bad night."

Davy put on his slicker and ate some cold biscuits and beans. He had some hot soup to get warm. "The wind is cold," Davy said.

Pa rode up to the chuck wagon. "We'll need every man in the saddle tonight," he said. "We can't let those longhorns stampede again."

"Do you want me to ride?" Davy asked.

Pa nodded. "I can use your help."

Davy pulled his hat lower over his eyes and rode out with the other cowboys.

Before midnight the rain turned to sleet. Davy could hear someone singing to keep the cattle calm. "Whoop-ee ti yi yo, get along little doggies!" If the longhorns stampeded in this storm, some could get lost and freeze before they were found.

It was the longest night Davy could ever remember. The sleet turned into snow. Davy couldn't even see Old Blue.

By daylight, the worst of the storm was over. The cowboys took turns eating breakfast. Davy stood by the fire trying to get warm.

"You okay, Davy?" Pa asked.

"Just cold," Davy told him.

"Do you want to ride in the wagon with Cookie?" Pa asked him.

Davy shook his head. "No, sir."

"Good boy, Davy. Cookie, how do you ever keep a fire going in all this snow?"

"That's my secret," Cookie said.

"Hey, look who's here," Davy said. Old Blue came close for a bit of Davy's biscuit. "Old Blue, I almost lost you last night," he said, rubbing the steer between his horns.

"When we get to Kansas City, I'm going to buy you a big bell to wear around your neck. Then I'll always know where you are," Davy said. "And so will the cattle."

"Nobody has ever belled a lead steer," Pa said. "But no steer was ever as tame as Old Blue. It's a good idea if it works."

"Davy, you don't have to wait until Kansas City. I've got a bell in the chuck wagon that you can use," Cookie told him. "I'll get it." He came back with a brass bell and a piece of rope.

Davy tied the bell around Old Blue's neck.
"There you go, Old Blue. How do you like that?"

Old Blue shook his horns and listened to the bell
clang. "Just look how proud that old steer is," said Pa,
laughing.

Davy gave Old Blue a hug. He shook his horns
again and rang the bell louder than before.

If a longhorn could smile, Old Blue would have.

Author's Note

Before the railroads reached into the cattle country of Texas, the only way of moving the cattle to market centers was by driving them over trails. Charles Goodnight, a famous trailblazer, owned a vast ranch inside the Palo Duro Canyon in the Texas Panhandle. His cattle were longhorns. The longhorns were the strongest and probably smartest cattle ever bred. They could cross thousands of miles, and their hard hooves showed no wear.

Sometimes a longhorn steer was born with an ability to lead the other cattle over trails. These lead cattle were highly valuable, and their owners never parted with them. Charles Goodnight owned one such steer named Old Blue. Of all the lead steers, Old Blue was surely the most remarkable. He was tame and was petted by all the cowboys.

The story told in this book concerns a trail drive which began at Goodnight's Palo Canyon ranch in Texas on October 26, 1878. During this drive Old Blue was given a brass bell to wear around his neck. Since lead steers were usually too wild to bell, Old Blue was the first to be so decorated. Cattle soon learned to listen for Old Blue's bell, and they always followed its clanging sound.

Old Blue led cattle from Texas to Kansas for eight years. Blue lived to be twenty years old, and his horns can be seen in a museum at Canyon, Texas.

Comprehension Check

Think and Discuss

1. What are three important things that happen to Davy and the cowboys on the trail drive?
• 2. Were you able to predict what the weather would be like during the following two months? Which details helped you make your prediction?
• 3. Did you predict that Old Blue would help the cowboys stop the stampede? Name the details that helped you make your prediction.
4. How do the cowboys use Old Blue to stop the cattle from stampeding?
5. If you were on a trail drive, which job would you like to have? Why?

• Comprehension: Predicting outcomes

Communication Workshop

Talk

Discuss with your classmates what other problems the cowboys might face during the rest of their journey.

Speaking/Listening: Cooperative learning

Write

Pretend you are riding along with Davy and Old Blue on the trail drive. Write a letter to a friend back home about one problem you face on your journey. Exchange letters with a classmate.

Writing Fluency: Friendly letter

Using a Telephone Directory

---

15   **BUTLER-CARLSON**

Camp World   2590 E. New York   **597-9150**
Cannon D   384 N. Summer Av   **598-6321**
Captain's Restaurant   519 E. Main   **597-7530**
Card Tim   755 Jackson **598-2921**
Carlson Betty   1520 Gates . .   **597-7873**
Carlson David   613 S. Garden Dr.   **597-7925**

The telephone directory, or phone book, has names, addresses, and telephone numbers of people and businesses. The names are listed in alphabetical order.

To find the name you need, use the guide words at the top of the page just like you do in a dictionary. To find a telephone number, look under the person's last name. Businesses are listed under the first word of the name.

Use this page from the telephone directory to answer these questions.

1. You need to rent equipment for a camping trip. What is Camp World's phone number?
2. You want to invite David Carlson to a ball game. What is his number?

*What does true friendship mean? A difficult
journey helps two friends answer that question.*

The Friendship of Damon and Pythias

by Plutarch

Retold by Nancy Ross Ryan

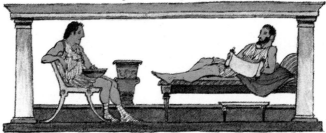

Long, long ago and far away there lived two
friends. One was named Damon. The other was
called Pythias. Damon and Pythias were the best of
friends. The story of their friendship has been told
and retold thousands of times.

Damon and Pythias are gone now. The city they
lived in is gone too. Yet, to this very day, the names
of Damon and Pythias stand for true friendship.

Damon and Pythias lived in a city ruled by the tyrant King Dionysius. A tyrant is a ruler whose word is law. A tyrant rules not by justice, but by power.

The proud and impatient King Dionysius was not really a bad man. But he was quick to anger and did not want to hear the ideas of others. The king was lonely and fearful. He was afraid that the people of the city would turn against him.

King Dionysius began to hear stories about young Pythias. The king's guards told him that Pythias often spoke in the town square. He spoke out against the king. He said the people did not need a king. He told the people that they could rule themselves. The townspeople were listening to Pythias and beginning to whisper to each other that his words made good sense.

Dionysius ordered his guards to bring Pythias before him. Pythias looked boldly at the king.

"Do you understand who I am?" Dionysius asked.

"Yes, mighty King, you are Dionysius," Pythias answered.

"Then why don't you bow to me?" the angry king asked.

"I don't believe that is proper," said Pythias. "It is not right for any man to bow to another. If I were king, I would not ask *you* to bow to *me*."

"It is not for you to decide what is right and proper. I am the king. My word is the law," the king shouted, his face red. "You do not obey me, so you must die!"

Even the king's guards were shocked at his words.

"Just because I would not bow, I must die!" Pythias cried.

The king was already sorry he had spoken in haste and anger, but he was too proud to change his mind.

"I have spoken. You must die," Dionysius said.

"Will you grant me one last wish?" Pythias asked. "Let me go to the village where my mother, father, sister, and sweetheart live. Let me say a last good-by to those I love. I will return before three weeks have ended and accept my fate."

"You must think me stupid!" the king said. "If I let you go, you will never come back."

"When I give my word, I keep it," replied Pythias.

The king just laughed a bitter laugh. The guards were about to take Pythias to the dungeon, when someone in the crowd spoke up.

"Put me in the dungeon," the voice said. "I will take the place of Pythias."

"Who speaks?" the king asked in surprise. A young man stepped up to the king.

"My name is Damon," he said. "Pythias is my friend. Let me take his place in the dungeon. Let him go to his village. He will come back as he promised."

"And if he doesn't?" the king asked Damon.

"Then I will die in his place," Damon said.

The king was amazed. He could not believe that someone would risk his life for a friend.

"All right. I will give you three weeks and not a minute more," he said to Pythias. "Now be off!"

The king turned to Damon and said, "If your friend is not back by noon three weeks from today, you will die." Then he told his guards to take Damon away.

The guards took Damon to the king's dungeon, a
natural pit in the ground. Called the Ear of
Dionysius, the pit was shaped like a trumpet,
narrow at the bottom and wide at the top. Because
of its shape, a word whispered at the bottom of
the pit could be heard clearly at the top.

The guards let Damon down into the pit on a
rope. Then they pulled up the rope and left Damon
alone in that deep, dark place.

The next morning the king woke up early. He went to the dungeon where Damon was being held. He was sure he would hear Damon crying with fear. But King Dionysius heard nothing.

Every day for a week King Dionysius went to the dungeon. Every day the king listened for sounds of suffering. But he heard nothing. He asked his guards if they had heard sad words from Damon.

"No, mighty Dionysius," guards answered. "As far as we know, Damon sleeps well, for we hear him lie down at night. We hear his quiet breathing. We hear him get up in the morning. He eats well too. The food basket we send down full comes up empty. Damon does not act as one who might die."

By the end of the week, King Dionysius could stand the silence no longer. He called down to Damon, "Aren't you sorry you took the place of Pythias? Aren't you afraid to die?"

"I will not die," Damon said softly. "I trust Pythias. He will return to take my place."

"Mark my words," said the king. "You will never see your friend again. Bring my chariot," the king roared to his guards. "Take me to the palace."

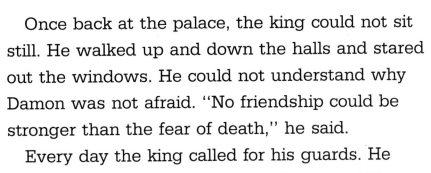

Once back at the palace, the king could not sit still. He walked up and down the halls and stared out the windows. He could not understand why Damon was not afraid. "No friendship could be stronger than the fear of death," he said.

Every day the king called for his guards. He asked them two questions. The first was, "Have you any word of Pythias?"

Day after day, the guards answered, "There is no word of Pythias, mighty King."

The second question the king asked was, "How is Damon resting?"

Day after day, the guards answered, "Damon is resting well, mighty King."

In his heart, King Dionysius admired Damon's loyalty to Pythias. He was sorry Damon would have to die. The king lost his taste for food. It was hard for him to sleep at night.

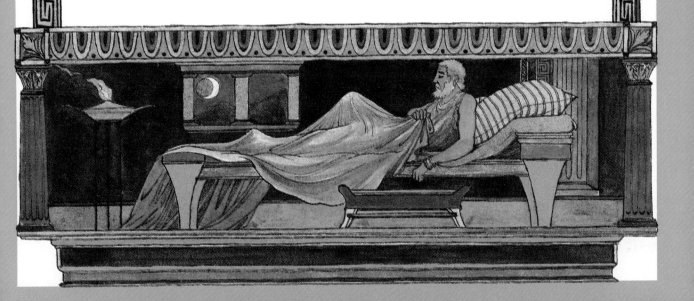

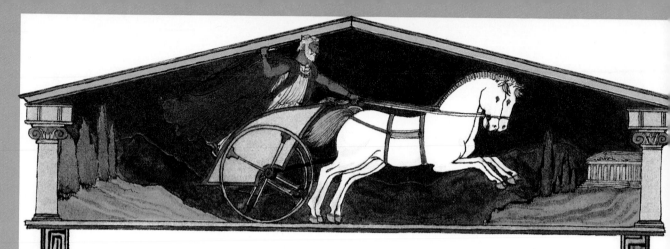

At the end of the second week, the king visited the dungeon again. When he came close to the edge of the pit, he heard no cries. He heard no moans. "The second week has passed, Damon," the king called. "Yet there is no word from your friend. Do you still trust him to return to save you from death?"

"I do," Damon answered.

"Do you not worry?" the king asked.

"I worry only that something may have happened to him," Damon answered. "If Pythias is well, he will return."

"Are you not sorry you took his place?" the king asked.

"I am sorry only that when Pythias returns, he will be put to death," Damon answered.

"Will you not beg for mercy?" the king asked.

"I beg you to let my friend live," Damon replied to the king.

"That is what you say today," the king said. "What will you say seven days from today, when the sundial points to noon? If Pythias is not back by then, you will beg for your life."

Every day for the next six days the king returned to the cave. Every day he called down to Damon and asked him the same questions. Every day Damon called up the same answers.

Finally the last day came. The sun was high in the sky. The king rode up in his chariot.

"Your time is almost up, Damon," the king called. "Yet Pythias is nowhere to be seen. Do you still think of him as your true friend?"

"I do," Damon answered.

"Do you not worry?" the king asked.

"I worry that something bad has happened to him," Damon answered. "If Pythias is able, he will surely return."

"Are you not sorry you took his place?" the king asked.

"I am sorry only when I think of Pythias returning too late to save me. I am sorry to think that I will not see my friend one last time."

"Will you not beg for mercy?" the king asked.

"I beg that when Pythias returns, you will let him live," Damon replied.

Damon was brought out of the dungeon. The guards tied his hands together with rope. "Foolish Damon," the king said. "The sundial points to noon. Your friend Pythias has not returned to save you. His promise was empty. He only wanted to save himself." The king turned to his guards and raised his hand.

"Wait, wait!" called a voice. It was Pythias. His clothes were torn and his skin was scratched. "I am here to accept my fate. Set Damon free."

For a moment no one spoke. Then Damon said to Pythias, "Good friend, I am both glad and sad to see you."

"Good friend," said Pythias to Damon, "I am both happy and unhappy to see you. This is hello and good-by."

"Silence!" the king ordered. "Why did you take so long to return?" he asked Pythias. "Let us hear your story."

"When I left the city, I rode to my village as fast as my horse would gallop," said Pythias. "My mother and father were overjoyed to see me. So were my sister and my sweetheart. When I said I must leave them, their smiles disappeared. When I told them why I must return, they began to cry. I explained that if I did not go back, Damon would die in my place. Then I kissed them all for the last time and started back with a heavy heart.

"My horse was frightened by a snake on a mountain path. The horse jumped suddenly and I fell off his back. My horse ran away before I could catch him. I didn't know it then, but that was not the end of my troubles.

"I started to walk. Since I had such a long way to go, I did not stop to sleep. I took only enough rest and food and water to keep me going. I thought of my poor friend in the dungeon and my promise to return.

"When I finally reached the river, I found that there had been a heavy rain. A flood had washed away the bridge. I walked until I found a narrow place in the river. Then I tried to swim across. Many times the flood waters washed me back to where I started. Many times I picked myself up and started across again. I was afraid I would not reach this city in time, but here I am at last."

When Pythias stopped talking, the king was silent. After a long time, he spoke. "I have never seen such a friendship in all my life. It would be a terrible thing to end your friendship in death. I pardon you, Pythias. You, too, Damon, are free to go. I would give all the gold in my palace for friends such as you."

"You cannot buy friendship," Damon said.

"But you may have it for free," said Pythias. "Come be our friend, we will be yours. The three of us will share the golden gift of friendship."

Meet the Author

The story of Damon and Pythias was written long ago by Plutarch (plü′ tärk). Plutarch was a writer best known for his *Lives,* a book about famous men from Greece and Rome. Through the years, many people have written stories, poems, and plays based on *Plutarch's Lives.*

Plutarch was born at Chaeronea (ker ə nē′ə), in Greece, more than a thousand years ago. He studied in Athens, Greece. Later he went to Rome to give talks.

Since there were no newspapers or photographs during his time, Plutarch had to travel far from home to gather information for his book. He collected facts and talked to people. Then he returned to Chaeronea to write *Lives.*

Plutarch's Lives tells about fifty great men. Plutarch wanted his readers to learn what the men were really like, not just what they did. His stories describe the men's thoughts and feelings about their lives. Plutarch tells where they were born, what their childhoods were like, what jobs they did, what their goals were, and how they died. Through Plutarch's stories, we learn not only about famous men's lives, but also what it was like to live in Greece and Rome during the long-ago times Plutarch wrote about.

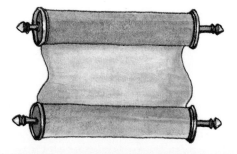

LOOKING BACK

Thinking and Writing About the Section

You've read about Evan, Davy, and Pythias—characters who journey near and far. Which character would be most interesting to travel with? You can write a persuasive paragraph to convince a partner of your opinion. First fill in this chart.

See your Thinker's Handbook for tips.

Character	Why He Is an Interesting Travel Companion
Evan	
Davy	
Pythias	

Writing

Choose your favorite character. Write a persuasive paragraph about why he would be the most interesting travel companion. State your opinion in the topic sentence and give at least two reasons to back it up. Your Writer's Handbook will provide more help.

Revising

Read your first draft to a partner. Do all the reasons support your opinion? Make changes, proofread, and write a final copy.

Presenting

Read your paragraph to your partner. Did you convince him or her?

Books to Read

The Stories Julian Tells by Ann Cameron

Julian is quite a storyteller. He uses his lively imagination to tell stories to his younger brother. You won't be able to keep yourself from laughing at the stories Julian tells.

Fooling Around with Words by Ruthven Tremain

Use this book and become a word detective. The book gives you lots of riddles and puzzles to solve.

A Matter of Pride by Emily Crofford

Hard times force Meg and her family to move to Arkansas so her father can find work. Life is hard in Arkansas, but Meg learns some lessons in the new place. One of the most important lessons she learns is about bravery.

Student's Handbooks

Writer's Handbook

Thinker's Handbook

Word Study Handbook

Glossary

351

This handbook answers questions you might ask yourself when you are writing. It will help you write the **Looking Back** assignments in this book as well as other writing assignments. It is divided into four parts: prewriting, writing, revising, and presenting. Each part tells about one step of the writing process. The handbook also explains these two types of writing: explanatory and persuasive/analytical.

Prewriting

1. **I know the topic I'm going to write about, but how can I organize my ideas and narrow my topic?**

One way is to use a chart, such as the one on page 125. Another way is to use a web, or cluster diagram. A cluster diagram shows at a glance how a main topic, subtopics, and details are related.

To make a cluster diagram, first write a main topic and circle it. Then write related subtopics around it. Circle them and draw lines to connect them to the main topic. Last, list details related to the subtopics.

Notice in the cluster diagram that the main topic is *Musical Instruments*. Coming out from the main topic are three narrower subtopics: *Stringed Instruments*, *Household Instruments*, and *Geraldine's Instrument*. The details that come from the subtopic *Household Instruments* are more narrow still.

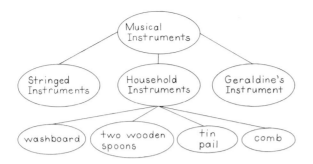

2. When I'm given a writing assignment, what is my first task?

When you receive a writing assignment, you should first decide on your *purpose* for writing and your *audience*. The people who will read your work are your audience. They may be your teacher, classmates, friends, family, or a writing partner. To determine your purpose, ask yourself: "What *type* of writing am I being asked to do?" Different types of writing have different purposes. Study the following chart to help you better understand your purpose for writing.

Type of Writing	Purpose	Examples
explanatory	• to tell how something is made or done • to tell the 5 w's—who, what, where, why, and when	• explanatory paragraph • news story • how-to report
persuasive/ analytical	• to state your opinion and give reasons in order to convince others to share your opinion • to analyze facts and reach a conclusion	• persuasive paragraph • book report • research report

Writing

1. Sometimes when I sit down, I just can't get started. What can I do then?

There are several ways to get started. Here are some suggestions.

<u>Prepare</u> Set aside about twenty minutes to write your first draft. Gather everything you need before you begin to write.

<u>Concentrate</u> Tell yourself you are not moving until you finish your first draft.

<u>Push Ahead</u> Sit down and pick up a pencil. Push your ideas out of your head and get them down on paper.

2. What is a first draft?

A first draft is like a trial run. First drafts give you a chance to get your ideas down. The writing and spelling does not have to be perfect. In fact, write a first draft as freely as you can. Write whatever comes to mind on your subject. Don't stop writing and don't worry about perfect spelling, punctuation, or capitalization. If you stop to correct these kinds of errors, you may lose your train of thought.

Revising

1. I have just written my first draft. What do I do next?

Take a minute to read over your first draft. "Listen" to yourself. Think about your big point. Is it clear? Will it make sense to your audience? Also ask yourself if your writing achieves the purpose you set. Have you really written the type of writing you were assigned? Does your draft reflect the steps in that kind of writing?

The chart below tells what can make each type of writing good.

Type of Writing	What Makes It Good
explanatory	• beginning with a topic sentence that tells what will be explained • following the topic sentence with details that support the main idea • telling the steps in order • making sure someone could follow the steps or understand the explanation • using examples to illustrate the steps
persuasive/ analytical	• keeping your audience in mind so you choose reasons and ideas that will appeal to them • beginning with a topic sentence that clearly states your opinion • using facts to support your opinion • drawing conclusions based on facts

2. What should I do when I revise?

First, revise your content. Have a writing conference by getting together with a small group, a partner, or your teacher. Read your draft aloud and ask what is good and what could be better. Take notes on the comments. They will help you make changes.

3. How do I make changes?

There are four kinds of changes to make when you revise: adding, taking out, reordering, and proofreading. Each one is explained below.

Adding Information Reread your draft. Check to see if you left out any important information. For example, do your facts support your opinion in your persuasive paragraph?

Taking Out Unnecessary Information Check to see that you have kept to your topic. Take out any sentences that don't belong. Also check for unnecessary words. Can you say the same thing in fewer words?

Moving Words, Sentences, and Paragraphs The order of your words, sentences, and paragraphs is what makes your writing clear. Have you told things in the right order? Do you need to move words or sentences?

Proofreading Finally, check your paper for mistakes in spelling, punctuation, capitalization, and form. Use the proofreading marks at the top of the next page.

Proofreader's Marks

$\equiv$	Make a capital.	✐	Take out something.
⊙	Add a period.	⌒→	Move something.
∧	Add something.	ⓢⓟ	Correct spelling.

4. How can I be sure I've done a thorough job of revising?

You can use this Revision Checklist to check yourself.

Revision Checklist

Content
- ✔ Did I say what I wanted to say?
- ✔ Are my details in order?
- ✔ Does my composition have a beginning, a middle, and an end?
- ✔ Is each paragraph about one main idea? Does the topic sentence state that main idea?
- ✔ Are any of the pronouns confusing?
- ✔ Have I taken out the unnecessary words?

Mechanics
- ✔ Does each sentence begin with a capital letter?
- ✔ Does each sentence end with the correct punctuation mark?
- ✔ Are other punctuation marks used correctly—such as commas and quotation marks?
- ✔ Do subjects and verbs agree?
- ✔ Did I keep the correct verb tense throughout?
- ✔ Did I capitalize proper nouns and adjectives?
- ✔ Did I check the spelling of difficult words?
- ✔ Is my handwriting clear and neat?

Presenting

1. What are some ways I can present my writing to others?

<u>Give an Oral Report</u> Read your paper aloud to your class. Practice beforehand by listening to yourself on a tape recorder.

<u>Draw Pictures</u> Draw pictures to illustrate your final draft. Mount it on construction paper. Then display your work on the classroom bulletin board.

<u>Type It</u> Use a computer or typewriter for your final draft. Then start a folder that contains your best pieces of writing. When the folder is full, type a Table of Contents for it.

<u>Make a Book</u> You can make a book that shows the shape of something you wrote about. Put your paper on a larger piece of paper and cut the shape you want. Add a cover and a back and tie your pages together.

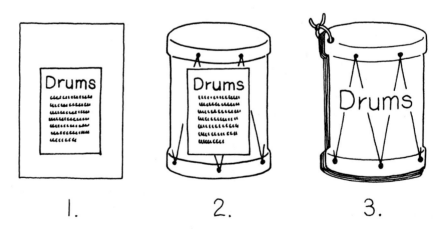

1.   2.   3.

2. **How can our class work together to present our writing?**

Here are some ways your class can work together.

<u>Hold a Contest</u> Follow these steps:

a. Join your classmates in submitting your best pieces of writing to a Class Writing Contest. (Your teacher can be the judge.)

b. As a class, decide on prizes for first, second, and third place winners.

c. All winning papers should be read aloud by the writers. Then they can be displayed with blue and red ribbons attached.

<u>Start a Class Newspaper</u> Follow these steps:

a. Choose a small group to be in charge of the newspaper.

b. As a class, think of a name for your newspaper. Then discuss the kinds of news stories, features, cartoons, and other articles you could include.

c. Decide when and how often you will publish.

d. Work in teams to revise and proofread all pieces.

e. Pass out the newspapers in and outside the school.

<u>Have a Circle Reading</u> Sit in circles with small groups. Hand your paper to the person on your right to read aloud.

This handbook can help you with your work assignments in *On Parade,* in other classes, and outside of school. It can help you think through tasks before, during, and after you do them. The handbook also includes several activities that may make you think in new ways.

Tips to Help You Think

Task 1: Understanding Content

To better understand what you read, think about questions like these:

- Is what I'm reading making sense? Should I reread?

- Can I figure out why the characters are acting the way they are?

- Can I identify the character's goal or problem and how the character is trying to solve it?

- Can I make a prediction about what will happen?

- Could I put this difficult passage in my own words?

- Would it help me to note causes, the order when things happen, or how they are alike or different?

- Can I state the point of this article?

- What main points do I need to include to talk about this article? What major events do I need to include to talk about this story?

Task 2: Answering Questions

To *answer* questions think about *asking* yourself questions such as these:

- Do I understand what this question is saying?

- Is this question asking for one or more answer?

- What other questions can I ask myself in order to lead up to this question?

- Would brainstorming for ideas help me get started?

- What do I need to do in order to get the answer to this kind of question?

Examples of Questions	Ways to Answer
What is the topic? List three facts.	Recall information that was stated *in* the selection
What happens in the story? What details support the main idea?	Gather and pull together several pieces of information.
What conclusion can you draw? What can you figure out from these facts?	Make inferences by using clues and your common sense to lead you to a decision.
Why is this a good title? Do you like the story? Why?	Evaluate, or judge, what you read and give examples.

Task 3: Communicating Ideas

When you work with a partner or a small group, keep these questions in mind:

• Do we have a clear idea about what we are to do?

• How should we organize ourselves? Should we each take a job or work together in committees?

• How should we proceed? Should we ask questions, role-play, or do steps in order?

• Do we need to break down the major goal into smaller steps?

• Would it help to put our information in a chart or web?

• Do we need to take notes on our ideas?

• Are we keeping to the task, or are we getting away from it?

• Are we asking others to make their ideas clear?

• Can we repeat in our own words what others are saying so we know we understand each other?

• Have we completed our task? Did we do what we set out to do?

Activities for You to Enjoy

Activity 1: Solving Problems

One way to solve problems is to evaluate, or judge, information. Think about questions such as the following as you read the paragraph below. Then tell what should be done.

- Do I have a clear idea of the overall problem?

- Would it help me to list each of the individual problems in this situation?

- How can I figure out which problem is the most serious to solve right away?

- Can I predict what might happen for my solutions?

- What solutions can I think of that could solve this problem?

Duke Stargazer and his sister Princess Lola had to make an emergency landing on a strange planet. They can repair their spaceship but it will take five hours. The temperature is freezing and frost is beginning to form inside the ship. Their zappers don't work and they see some creatures approaching. Their supplies include some food packets, one working computer, and some balloons their crew gave Duke for his birthday. Duke feels dizzy everytime he stands up and Lola is finding it hard to breathe. The creatures are now right outside the hatch. What should be done?

Activity 2: Making Decisions

One way to make decisions is to think about what choices you have. Think about questions like the ones below as you read the paragraph. Then help Chiyo make decisions.

• Do I know what decision I need to make?

• How many choices do I have? Would it help me to list them?

• Would it help me to compare what I know to the choices I have?

• What are my restrictions—things that rule out certain choices?

This summer Chiyo gets to go to a special camp. The camp offers many activities but she can only sign up for three. Chiyo isn't a very good swimmer and that worries her because she lives by the ocean. She loves baseball and soccer and has played them for two years at school. Chiyo is a good leader and is president of the art club. Chiyo also loves doing new things. The camp offers swimming, baseball, soccer, coaching, crafts, music, and writing. She must mail her choices to the camp today. What decisions should she make?

Activity 3: Asking the Right Questions

One way to ask the right kind of questions is to think about *why* you need to ask them. Read the tips below and use them to help Mr. Nichols.

- Think about your main purpose in asking questions.

- Decide which things are important for you to know.

- Think about information you already know and see if you can use it to ask what you don't know.

- Decide which questions will lead you to get the information you need.

When a group of thirty hikers discovered a hidden mountain lake, several of the adults and children wanted to swim. The guide, Mr. Nichols, could not swim. Mr. Nichols knew that swimming would be a refreshing break on a hot day, but he wanted to make sure everyone would be safe. What questions would be helpful for him to ask?

How deep is the water?

Does any adult in the group have experience as a life guard?

What name can we call this lake?

How well can each child swim?

How many different kinds of fish are in the lake?

Is there a strong undercurrent in the water?

Is there a sandy beach for building sand castles?

Activity 4: Determining Relevance of Information

One way to determine the relevance of information is to figure out if it is relevant—necessary to your task—or irrelevant—not necessary or helpful. Read these questions and use them to help Detective Spade.

- Can I identify the task?

- Would it help me to list all my requirements?

- Can I trace where each piece of information might take me in order to figure out if it is relevant?

- Can I list the information that is not relevant?

- Can I explain what information is relevant?

Sue Spade, a famous detective, has been asked to investigate the disappearance of the Cockroaches' gold record. These are the notes she took:

     last seen on wall in studio yesterday at noon
     only the Cockroaches and the cleaning staff have
       keys to the studio
     there are three stereos in the studio
     Dingo Cockroach has red hair
     the tape recorder was left on last night
     the group has been together for five years

Sue thinks some of this information is helpful. Which notes are helpful?

On the next few pages are some of the strategies you've learned to figure out the meaning and pronunciation of words.

Phonics: Consonant Blends and Digraphs

Strategy 1: I can use what I know about consonants and **consonant blends and digraphs.**

Say these words. Listen to the sounds of the letters blended together or the letters that stand for one sound at the beginning or end of a word.

drew	**b**oa**st**	**sh**all	hu**ng**
stalk	s**c**o**ld**	**ch**alk	clo**th**
slump	e**rr**and	**th**um**b**	tou**gh**
scroll	su**gg**est	**wh**i**stle**	appro**ach**

Vocabulary and Skill Application

Write the sentences. Use the words from the box to complete the sentences.

1. Everyone thought Bob ____ a terrific picture.
2. He used different pieces of colored ____.
3. The teacher ____ his picture on the wall.
4. Bob didn't ____ to anyone about his picture.
5. Bob wanted to ____ an idea for a class picture.
6. He decided to ____ the teacher with his new idea.
7. She thought it would be fun to draw on ____.
8. The class could roll the cloth to make a ____.

Phonics: Consonants and Context

Strategy 2: I can use what I know about **consonants and context.**

Read the sentence and the words.
   The game directions were s mpl to understand.
      easy   <u>simple</u>   sample
Which of the three words might make sense in the sentence? Which of the three words match the consonants in the unfinished word? Which of the words makes sense and has consonants that match those of the unfinished word?

Vocabulary and Skill Application

Write the sentences. Use the meaning of the surrounding words in each sentence and the consonants in the unknown words to figure out the unfinished word.

1. The train carried the <u>fr   ght</u> to the city.
   boxes   fright   freight
2. The princess lives in a <u>p l c</u> by the lake.
   castle   police   palace
3. The water started to <u>p   r</u> over the rocks.
   flow   pour   pair
4. The coach tried not to <u>b   st</u> about his team.
   talk   beast   boast
5. Mrs. Lee has a dance <u>st d</u> in her home.
   room   studio   steady

Phonics: Short Vowel Sounds

Strategy 3: I can use what I know about **short vowel sounds.**

Say these words. Listen to the vowel sounds. What kind of letters are before and after the vowel in each word?

Short *a*	Short *e*	Short *i*	Short *o*	Short *u*
camp	lens	brim	solve	shrug
rather	fence	film	common	crumb
chatter	lever	simple	promise	budge
banquet	twelve	glimpse	involve	thumb

Vocabulary and Skill Application

Write the sentences. Use the words from the box to complete the sentences.

1. There were _____ of us waiting for the bus.
2. I caught a _____ of the bus around the corner.
3. So many people were on the bus we could not _____.
4. A crowded bus is a _____ problem in the morning.
5. I decided to _____ my problem by riding my bike.
6. I would _____ ride my bike than ride on the bus.
7. The next day I rode my bike to the theater to see a _____.
8. On the way I fell on my hand and broke my _____.
9. One _____ in my glasses broke too.
10. My bike hit a picket _____.
11. How could riding a bike be both _____ and hard?
12. I made a _____ to be careful when I ride my bike.

Phonics: Long Vowel Sounds

Strategy 4: I can use what I know about **long vowel sounds.**

Say these words. Listen to the vowel sounds. Which words have two vowels together that stand for a long vowel sound? Which words have a vowel and a consonant followed by the letter *e*?

Long *a*	Long *e*	Long *i*	Long *o*	Long *u*
tape	sleep	knife	zone	rule
frame	creak	might	boast	tune
break	scene	alive	lonely	truce
freight	series	thrive	approach	excuse

Vocabulary and Skill Application

Write the sentences. Use the words from the box to complete the sentences.

1. Dad knew I would be _____ while I was sick.
2. So Dad thought I _____ enjoy a surprise.
3. He brought me a picture in a beautiful _____.
4. The picture was a _____ from my favorite book.
5. Dad also brought home a music _____.
6. We sang a _____ from the tape.
7. Then I watched my favorite TV _____.
8. Dad liked to _____ that it was his favorite too.
9. We have a _____ about watching TV at night.
10. Dad said we could _____ the rule just this once.
11. When the show was over I had to go to _____.
12. Dad wrote an _____ because I had missed school.

Phonics: R-Controlled Vowels

Strategy 5: I can use what I know about **r-controlled vowels.**

Say these words. Listen to the vowel sounds. What letter comes after the vowel in each word?

card	her	stir	wore	hurt
start	were	firm	work	turn
alarm	term	first	force	cure
large	serve	circle	porch	burnt
starve	sternly	squirm	horse	hurdle

Vocabulary and Skill Application

Write the sentences. Use the words from the box to complete the sentences.

1. For the _____ time Jo cooked a meal for us.
2. Her mom listed the cooking rules on a _____.
3. Jo tried to follow _____ mom's directions.
4. Jo was careful about what she _____ in the kitchen.
5. Mom said _____, "Be careful when you cook!"
6. Jo said she would _____ to _____ dinner soon.
7. Suddenly, the smoke _____ went off in the kitchen.
8. Smoke began to _____ the living room.
9. The food was _____ around the edges.
10. The roast was not _____ anymore.
11. Jo had to throw out all of her hard _____.
12. The family tried not to _____ her feelings.
13. We didn't want to _____, so we went out to eat.

Phonics: Vowel Sounds

Strategy 6: I can use what I know about **vowel sounds.**

Say these words. Listen to the vowel sounds. What letters stand for the vowel sounds in each word?

loud	owl	boy
proud	know	join
bought	show	enjoy
brought	clown	noise
drought	shallow	hoist

Vocabulary and Skill Application

Write the sentences. Use the words from the box to complete the sentences.

1. I'm not the only ____ in town who plays ball.
2. All the children in our town want to ____ a team.
3. We ____ playing baseball.
4. I play second base in the ____ part of the field.
5. Each year we have to ____ the coach what we ____.
6. The coach's voice is ____ during practice.
7. He makes the most ____ when we play a game.
8. The coach doesn't allow us to ____ around.
9. One day he ____ new baseball clothes for us.
10. He ____ them to practice.
11. Every child had an ____ on his baseball cap.
12. We were so ____ of our new clothes.

Structure: Syllabication

Strategy 7: I can use what I know about **syllabication.**

A. When a word ends in *-le,* divide before the consonant: sim/ple, whis/tle
B. When a word has two consonants between two vowels, divide between the two consonants:
         suf/fer, dis/tant
C. When a word has one consonant between two vowels, divide before or after the consonant:
         he/ro, liz/ard

Vocabulary and Skill Application

Write the sentences. Use the words from the list to complete the sentences.

common	alarm	design	famine
promise	simple	linger	content
nonsense	jungle	advance	dessert

1. Sue made a ____ to practice piano each day.
2. There can be no ____ when she practices.
3. She has played very ____ music for a long time.
4. Now Sue wants to ____ to harder music.

Structure: Prefixes and Suffixes

Strategy 8: I can use what I know about **prefixes and suffixes.**

See Skill Lesson: Prefixes *Over-, Under-* on pages 141-142.

Etymologies: Word Histories
Strategy 9: I can use what I know about **word histories.**

See Skill Lesson: Learning About Word Histories on pages 260-261.

Word Study: Dictionary
Strategy 10: I can use the dictionary to find pronunciations and meanings of words.

grudge	guillotine			
a hat	**i** it	**oi** oil	**ch** child	**ə** stands for:
ā age	**ī** ice	**ou** out	**ng** long	a in about
ä far	**o** hot	**u** cup	**sh** she	e in taken
				i in pencil

guide (gīd), **1** show the way; lead; direct: *The scout guided us through the wilderness.* **2** person or thing that shows the way: *Tourists sometimes hire guides.* 1 *verb,* **guid•ed, guid•ing; 2** *noun.*

Vocabulary and Skill Application
Write and answer the questions below.

1. What shows the first and last word on a page?
2. What shows how the letter sounds?
3. What do you call the word you are looking for?
4. Which definition gives you the meaning for the underlined word in the following sentence?
   The <u>guide</u> took us through the cave.

Glossary

How to Use the Pronunciation Key

After each entry word in this glossary, there is a special spelling, called the **pronunciation**. It shows how to say the word. The word is broken into syllables and then spelled with letters and signs. You can look up these letters and signs in the **pronunciation key** to see what sounds they stand for.

This dark mark (′) is called the **primary accent**. It follows the syllable you say with the most force. This lighter mark (′) is the **secondary accent**. Say the syllable it follows with medium force. Syllables without marks are said with least force.

Full Pronunciation Key

a	hat, cap	i	it, pin	p	paper, cup	ə	stands for:
ā	age, face	ī	ice, five	r	run, try		a in about
ä	father, far			s	say, yes		e in taken
		j	jam, enjoy	sh	she, rush		i in pencil
b	bad, rob	k	kind, seek	t	tell, it		o in lemon
ch	child, much	l	land, coal	th	thin, both		u in circus
d	did, red	m	me, am	ŦH	then, smooth		
		n	no, in				
e	let, best	ng	long, bring	u	cup, butter		
ē	equal, be			u̇	full, put		
ėr	her, learn	o	hot, rock	ü	rule, move		
		ō	open, go				
f	fat, if	ô	order, all	v	very, save		
g	go, bag	oi	oil, toy	w	will, woman		
h	he, how	ou	house, out	y	young, yet		
				z	zoo, breeze		
				zh	measure, seizure		

The contents of the Glossary entries in this book have been adapted from *Scott, Foresman Beginning Dictionary*, Copyright © 1983 Scott, Foresman and Company.

A

ac·ci·dent (ak′sə dənt), something harmful or unlucky that happens: *She was hurt in a car accident. noun.*

ache (āk), **1** constant pain: *My cousin ate too much food and got a stomach ache.* **2** be in pain; hurt: *My arm aches.* **3** be eager; wish very much: *During the hot days of August we all ached to go swimming.* **1** *noun,* 2,3 *verb,* **ached, ach·ing.**

ad·ap·ta·tion (ad′ap tā′shən), something made by changing to fit different conditions: *A play is often an adaptation of a book. noun.*

ad·vance (ad vans′), move forward: *The angry crowd advanced toward the building. verb,* **ad·vanced, ad·vanc·ing.**

a·far (ə fär′), from afar, from far off; from a distance: *I saw them from afar. adverb.*

a·gainst (ə genst′), **1** in opposition to: *It is against the law to cross the street when the light is red.* **2** upon: *Rain beats against the window. preposition.*

a·larm (ə lärm′), **1** sudden fear; excitement caused by fear of danger: *The deer darted off in alarm.* **2** make afraid; frighten: *The breaking of a branch under my foot alarmed the deer.* **3** a bell or other device that makes noise to warn or awaken people. 1,3 *noun,* 2 *verb.*

a·lert (ə lėrt′), **1** wide-awake: *The dog was alert to every sound.* **2** lively: *An owl is very alert in its movements.* **3** warn. 1,2 *adjective,* 3 *verb.*

a·live (ə līv′), **1** having life; living: *Was the snake alive or dead?* **2** active: *All winter we kept our hopes alive for a warm spring. adjective.*

al·to·geth·er (ôl′tə geᴛн′ər), **1** completely; entirely: *The house was altogether destroyed by fire.* **2** on the whole: *Altogether, he was pleased. adverb.*

an·nounce (ə nouns′), **1** give public or formal notice of: *Please announce to the children that there will be no school today.* **2** make known the presence or arrival of: *The loudspeaker announced each airplane as it landed. verb,* **an·nounced, an·nounc·ing.**

ap·proach (ə prōch′), come near or nearer: *Walk softly as you approach the baby's crib. verb,* **ap·proached, ap·proach·ing.**

a·side (ə sīd′), **1** to one side; away: *He stepped aside to let me pass.* **2** words spoken by an actor and heard by the audience which the other persons on the stage are not supposed to hear. 1 *adverb,* 2 *noun.*

as·ton·ish (ə ston′ish), surprise greatly: *The gift of ten dollars astonished me. verb.*

au·to·graph (ô′tə graf), **1** a person's signature: *Many people collect the autographs of actors.* See picture. **2** write one's name in or on. 1 *noun,* 2 *verb.*

B

back·ground (bak′ground′), the part of a picture or scene toward the back: *The picture had mountains in the background. noun.*

bac·ter·i·a (bak tir′ ē ə), very tiny and simple plants, so small that they can usually be seen only through a microscope. See picture. *noun.*

bal·let (bal′ā), **1** a kind of dance by a group on a stage. A ballet usually tells a story through the movements of the dancing and the music. **2** the dancers: *The Royal Ballet will soon perform in our city. noun.*

ba·nan·a (bə nan′ə), a curved, yellow fruit that grows on a tree. Bananas are five to eight inches long and grow in large bunches. *noun.*

autograph

bacteria as seen through a microscope

ban·quet (bang′kwit), a large meal prepared for a special event or for many people; feast: *a wedding banquet. noun.*

bare (ber *or* bar), **1** without covering; not clothed; naked: *The sun burned his bare shoulders.* **2** empty; not furnished: *a room bare of furniture. adjective.*

bar·gain (bär′gən), **1** agreement to trade or exchange: *You can't back out on our bargain.* **2** something offered for sale cheap: *This hat is a bargain.* **3** try to make a good deal: *I bargained with the shopkeeper and bought the book for $2 instead of $5.* 1,2 *noun,* 3 *verb.*

blind·fold (blīnd′fōld′), **1** cover the eyes of: *We blindfolded her.* **2** with the eyes covered: *He walked the line blindfolded.* **3** thing covering the eyes. 1 *verb,* 2 *adjective,* 3 *noun.*

boast (bōst), **1** speak too highly of oneself or what one owns: *He boasts about his grades.* **2** statement speaking too highly of oneself or what one owns; boasting words: *I don't believe her boasts about how fast she can run.* 1 *verb,* 2 *noun.*

brim (brim), the edge of a hat: *The hat's wide brim shaded my eyes from the sun. noun.*

budge (buj), move even a little: *The stone was so heavy that we couldn't budge it. verb,* **budged, budg·ing.**

buf·fa·lo (buf′ə lō), a wild ox with a great shaggy head and strong front legs. Herds of buffaloes used to graze on the plains of the United States. *noun, plural* **buf·fa·loes, buf·fa·los,** *or* **buf·fa·lo.**

C

cam·er·a (kam′ər ə), instrument for taking motion pictures or photographs. See picture. *noun.*

cap·i·tal (kap′ə təl), city where the government of a country or state is located. Washington is the capital of the United States. Each state of the United States has a capital. *noun.*

car·riage (kar′ij), vehicle that moves on wheels. Some carriages are pulled by horses and are used to carry people. Baby carriages are small and light, and can often be folded. *noun.*

cause (kôz), **1** person, thing, or event that makes something happen: *The flood was the cause of much damage.* **2** make happen; make do; bring about: *A loud noise caused me to jump.* 1 *noun,* 2 *verb,* **caused, caus·ing.**

chalk (chôk), a soft writing tool for marking on a blackboard. *noun.*

char·ac·ter (kar′ik tər), person or animal in a play, poem, story, or book: *My favorite character in Charlotte's Web is Wilbur, the pig. noun.*

char·i·ot (char′ē ət), a two-wheeled cart pulled by horses. The chariot was used long ago for fighting and racing. *noun.*

chat·ter (chat′ər), **1** talk quickly and without stopping about unimportant things: *The children chattered about the circus.* **2** make quick, unclear sounds: *Monkeys chatter. verb.*

cheer·ful (chir′fəl), joyful; glad: *She is a smiling, cheerful girl. adjective.*

chim·pan·zee (chim′pan zē′ *or* chim pan′zē), an African ape smaller than a gorilla. Chimpanzees are very smart. *noun.*

chord (kôrd), two or more notes of music sounded at the same time. *noun.*

cho·rus (kôr′əs), **1** group of singers who sing together: *Our school chorus sang at the town hall.* See picture. **2** sing or speak all at the same time: *The birds were chorusing around me.* 1 *noun, plural* **cho·rus·es;** 2 *verb.*

a hat	oi oil	ə stands for:
ā age	ou out	a in about
ä far	u cup	e in taken
e let	u̇ put	i in pencil
ē equal	ü rule	o in lemon
ėr term	ch child	u in circus
i it	ng long	
ī ice	sh she	
o hot	th thin	
ō open	ᴛʜ then	
ô order	zh measure	

camera
motion picture **camera**

chorus

dawn

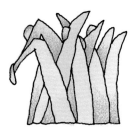

dew—Dew covered the grass in the morning.

chuck wag·on (chuk′wag′ən), (in the western United States) a wagon or truck that carries food and cooking tools for cowhands or harvest workers. *noun.*

cloth (klôth), material made from wool, cotton, silk, or other fiber. Cloth is used for clothing, curtains, bedding, and many other things. *noun, plural* **cloths.**

co·in·ci·dence (kō in′sə dəns), two things happening at the same time, by chance. *It is a coincidence that my cousin and I were born on the same day. noun.*

con·tent (kən tent′), **1** please: *Nothing contents me when I am sick.* **2** pleased: *I will be content to stay at home.* **1** *verb,* **2** *adjective.*

con·tin·ue (kən tin′yü), keep up; keep on: *The rain continued all day. verb,* **con·tin·ued, con·tin·u·ing.**

court (kôrt), **1** place where people go to be put on trial: *The prisoner was brought to court for trial.* **2** place where a king, queen, or other ruler lives. *noun.*

court·yard (kôrt′yärd′), space enclosed by walls, in or near a large building. *noun.*

creak (krēk), **1** squeak loudly: *The hinges on the door creaked because they needed oiling.* **2** creaking noise: *The creak of the stairs in the old house was spooky.* **1** *verb,* **2** *noun.*

cre·ate (krē āt′), **1** make a thing which has not been made before: *Composers create music.* **2** be the cause of: *The noise created a problem. verb,* **cre·at·ed, cre·at·ing.**

crumb (krum), very small piece of bread or other food broken from a larger piece: *I fed crumbs to the birds. noun.*

cure (kyùr), **1** bring back to health; make well: *The medicine cured the sick child.* **2** get rid of: *cure a cold.* **3** something that gets rid of a disease: *a cure for a cold.* **1,2** *verb,* **cured, cur·ing; 3** *noun.*

cur·i·ous (kyùr′ē əs), **1** eager to know: *Small children are very curious.* **2** strange: *I found a curious old box in the attic. adjective.*

D

dawn (dôn), beginning of day. See picture. *noun.*

de·li·cious (di lish′əs), very pleasing to the taste or smell: *a delicious cake. adjective.*

des·per·ate (des′pər it), **1** ready to run any risk: *a desperate robber.* **2** having little chance for hope or cure; very dangerous: *a desperate illness. adjective.*

de·tec·tive (di tek′tiv), **1** member of a police force or other person whose work is finding information secretly and solving crimes. **2** having something to do with detectives and their work: *She likes reading detective stories.* **1** *noun,* **2** *adjective.*

dew (dü *or* dyü), small drops of water that form on cool places during the night. See picture. *noun.*

di·a·gram (dī′ə gram), drawing or sketch showing important parts of a thing. A plan of a house or a ship is a diagram. *noun.*

dig·ni·fied (dig′nə fīd), having pride and self-respect: *The queen has a dignified manner. adjective.*

di·rec·tor (də rek′tər), manager; person who directs. *noun.*

dis·as·ter (də zas′tər), event that causes much suffering or loss. A flood, fire, shipwreck, earthquake, or great loss of money is a disaster. *noun.*

dis·cov·er (dis kuv′ər), find out; see or learn of for the first time: *I discovered their secret. verb.*

dis·ease (də zēz′), **1** sickness; illness: *People, animals, and plants can all suffer from disease.* **2** any kind of illness: *Measles and chicken pox are two diseases of children. noun.*

dis·gust (dis gust′), **1** strong dislike; sickening dislike: *We feel disgust for bad odors or tastes.* **2** cause a feeling of disgust in: *The smell of rotten eggs disgusts many people.* **1** *noun,* **2** *verb.*

dis·tant (dis′tənt), **1** far away in space: *The sun is distant from us.* **2** not close: *We plan a trip to Europe in the distant future. adjective.*

dol·phin (dol′fən), a sea mammal much like a small whale. It has a snout like a beak and is very smart. *noun.*

drought (drout), **1** a long period of dry weather: *The drought lasted 12 weeks.* **2** lack of water; dryness. See picture. *noun.*

dun·geon (dun′jən), a dark underground room or cell to keep prisoners in. *noun.*

E

ease (ēz), **1** freedom from pain or trouble. **2** make easy; loosen: *The belt is too tight; ease it a little.* **1,** *noun,* **2** *verb,* **eased, eas·ing.**

ech·o (ek′ō), a repeated sound. You hear an echo when a sound you make bounces back from a distant hill or wall so that you hear it again. *noun, plural* **ech·oes.**

edge (ej), **1** line or place where something ends; part farthest from the middle; side: *This page has four edges.* **2** the thin side that cuts: *The knife had a very sharp edge. noun.*

e·lect (i lekt′), **1** choose by voting: *Americans elect a President every four years.* **2** choose: *She elected to study math. verb,* **e·lect·ed, e·lect·ing.**

e·lec·tric (i lek′trik), having something to do with electricity: *an electric light. adjective.*

e·nor·mous (i nôr′məs), very, very large; huge: *Long ago enormous animals lived on the earth. adjective.*

e·quip·ment (i kwip′mənt), outfit; supplies: *We keep our camping equipment in order. noun.*

er·rand (er′ənd), **1** trip to do something: *She has gone on an errand to the store.* **2** what one is sent to do: *I did ten errands in one trip. noun.*

es·pe·cial·ly (e spesh′ə lē), more than others; chiefly; mainly: *This book is especially written for students. adverb.*

ex·am·ple (eg zam′pəl), **1** sample; one thing taken to show what the others are like: *New York is an example of a busy city.* **2** model; pattern: *Children often follow the example set by their parents.* **3** problem in arithmetic: *She wrote the example on the board. noun.*

ex·claim (ek sklām′), cry out; speak suddenly in surprise or strong feeling: *"Here you are at last!" I exclaimed. verb.*

ex·cuse (ek skyüz′ *for 1,3,4;* ek skyüs′ *for 2*), **1** try to remove the blame of: *She excused her lateness by blaming traffic.* **2** reason, real or pretended, that is given: *He had many excuses for coming late.* **3** be a reason for: *Sickness excuses staying home from school.* **4** pardon; forgive: *Excuse me; I have to go now.* **1,3,4** *verb,* **ex·cused, ex·cus·ing; 2** *noun.*

ex·haust·ed (eg zô′stid), worn out; very tired: *The exhausted hikers rested after their long walk.* See picture. *adjective.*

F

fab·u·lous (fab′yə ləs), beyond belief; amazing: *Ten dollars is a fabulous price for a pencil. adjective.*

fam·ine (fam′ən), **1** lack of food in a place; a time of starving: *Many people died during the famine in India.* **2** starvation: *Many people died of famine. noun.*

fan·tas·tic (fan tas′tik), very odd; unreal; strange and wild in shape or manner: *The firelight cast strange, fantastic shadows on the walls. adjective.*

a hat	oi oil	ə stands for:
ā age	ou out	a in about
ä far	u cup	e in taken
e let	ů put	i in pencil
ē equal	ü rule	o in lemon
ėr term	ch child	u in circus
i it	ng long	
ī ice	sh she	
o hot	th thin	
ō open	ᴛʜ then	
ô order	zh measure	

drought—Crops can die during a **drought.**

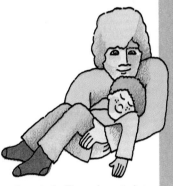

exhausted—The **exhausted** child fell asleep in her mother's arms.

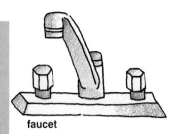

faucet

garage

gnaw—Puppies like to **gnaw** slippers.

fau·cet (fô′sit), device for turning on or off a flow of liquid from a pipe or a container holding it; tap. See picture. *noun.*

fer·ry (fer′ē), a boat used to carry passengers and vehicles across a body of water. *noun, plural* **fer·ries.**

film (film), **1** roll or sheet of thin material covered with a coating that is changed by light, used to take photos: *He bought two rolls of film for his camera.* **2** motion picture: *We saw a film about animals.* **3** make a motion picture of: *They filmed "The Wizard of Oz."* **4** photograph or be photographed for motion pictures: *They filmed the scene three times.* 1,2 *noun,* 3,4 *verb.*

fir·ma·ment (fèr′mə mənt), the sky. *noun.*

folk (fōk), people: *Most city folk know very little about farming. noun, plural* **folk** or **folks.**

force (fôrs), **1** power; strength: *The speeding car struck the tree with great force.* **2** group of people who work together: *our office force, police force.* **3** get or take by strength: *He forced his way in.* 1,2 *noun,* 3 *verb,* **forced, forc·ing.**

freight (frāt), **1** goods that a train, truck, ship, or aircraft carries. **2** the carrying of goods on a train, ship, aircraft, or truck: *He sent the box by freight.* **3** train or ship for carrying goods. *noun.*

G

ga·rage (gə räzh′), **1** place where cars are kept. **2** shop for fixing cars. See picture. *noun.*

gar·bage (gär′bij), scraps of food to be thrown away from a kitchen, dining room, or store. *noun.*

gi·gan·tic (jī gan′tik), big like a giant; huge: *An elephant is a gigantic animal. adjective.*

glimpse (glimps), **1** short look: *I caught a glimpse of the waterfall as our train went by.* **2** catch a brief view of: *I glimpsed the waterfall as our train went by.* 1 *noun,* 2 *verb,* **glimpsed, glimps·ing.**

gnaw (nô), bite at and wear away: *A mouse has gnawed right through the cover of this box.* See picture. *verb.*

gov·er·nor (guv′ər nər), **1** person elected as the head of a state of the United States. The governor of a state carries out the laws made by the state legislature. **2** ruler of a province, colony, city, or fort. *noun.*

guard (gärd), **1** watch over; take care of; keep safe; defend: *The dog guarded the child day and night.* **2** person or group that protects or watches. A soldier or group of soldiers protecting a person or place is a guard. 1 *verb,* 2 *noun.*

guest (gest), visitor: *He was a guest at the motel. noun.*

guide (gīd), **1** show the way; lead; direct: *The scout guided us through the woods.* **2** person or thing that shows the way: *Tourists sometimes hire guides.* 1 *verb,* **guid·ed, guid·ing;** 2 *noun.*

gui·tar (gə tär′), a musical instrument having six strings, played with the fingers or with a pick. *noun.*

guy (gī), a man or boy: *noun.*

H

her·o (hir′ō), **1** person admired for bravery, great deeds, or noble qualities. **2** the most important male person in a story, play, or poem. *noun, plural* **her·oes.**

hic·cough (hik′up), a sudden intake of breath with a muffled clicking sound. *noun.*

hoarse (hôrs), **1** sounding rough and deep: *the hoarse sound of the bullfrog.* **2** having a rough voice: *A bad cold can make you hoarse. adjective,* **hoars·er, hoars·est.**

hoist (hoist), **1** lift up: *She hoisted the flag.* **2** lift: *She gave me a hoist up the wall.* 1 *verb,* 2 *noun.*

hop·scotch (hop′skoch′), a children's game in which the players hop over the lines of a figure drawn on the ground. *noun.*

hor·ror (hôr′ər), a shivering, shaking terror: *She had a look of horror on her face. noun.*

hov·er (huv′ər), **1** stay in or near one place in the air: *The two birds hovered over their nest.* **2** stay in or near one place; wait nearby: *The dogs hovered around the kitchen door at mealtime. verb.*

I

im·mense (i mens′), very big; huge; vast: *An ocean is an immense body of water. adjective.*

in·cog·ni·to (in′kog nē′tō), changed appearance to avoid being recognized: *He traveled incognito. adverb.*

in·for·ma·tion (in′fər mā′shən), things known; facts: *A dictionary contains much information about words. noun.*

in·jure (in′jər), do damage to; harm; hurt: *Do not break or injure the bushes in the park. verb,* **in·jured, in·jur·ing.**

in·stru·ment (in′strə mənt), **1** thing used to do something; tool: *A drill is an instrument used by dentists.* **2** device for producing musical sounds: *wind instruments, string instruments. A violin, cello, and piano were the instruments played. noun.*

in·tro·duce (in′trə düs′, *or* in′ trə dyüs′), **1** bring in: *She introduced a story into the conversation.* **2** make known: *Mrs. Brown, may I introduce Mr. Smith?* **3** begin: *He introduced his speech by telling a joke. verb,* **in·tro·duced, in·tro·duc·ing.**

in·vis·i·ble (in viz′ə bəl), not capable of being seen: *Germs are invisible to the naked eye. adjective.*

in·vi·ta·tion (in′və tā′shən), a polite request to come to some place or to do something. *The children received invitations to the party. noun.*

in·volve (in volv′), **1** have as a necessary part; include: *Housework involves cooking, washing dishes, sweeping, and cleaning.* **2** bring (into difficulty or danger): *One foolish mistake can involve you in a good deal of trouble.* **3** take up the attention of: *She was involved in working out a puzzle. verb,* **in·volved, in·volv·ing.**

J

jade (jād), a hard stone used for jewelry and ornaments. Most jade is green. See picture. *noun.*

jus·tice (jus′tis), **1** fair dealing: *Judges should have a sense of justice.* **2** fairness; rightness; being just: *She never doubted the justice of the king. noun.*

jade

K

key (kē), **1** a small metal instrument for fastening and unfastening the lock of a door, a padlock, or any other thing. **2** one of a set of parts pressed in playing a piano or other instrument: *Don't hit the keys so hard. noun.*

L

law·yer (lô′yər), person who knows the laws and gives advice about matters of law or acts for another person in court. *noun.*

la·zi·ly (lā′zə lē), in a lazy manner. *adverb.*

leg·end (lej′ənd), **1** story coming down from the past, which many people have believed: *The stories about Robin Hood are legends, not history.* **2** such stories as a group. *noun.*

a hat	oi oil	ə stands for:
ā age	ou out	a in about
ä far	u cup	e in taken
e let	ù put	i in pencil
ē equal	ü rule	o in lemon
ėr term	ch child	u in circus
i it	ng long	
ī ice	sh she	
o hot	th thin	
ō open	ŧH then	
ô order	zh measure	

leopard

longhorn

mesquite

mobile

lens (lenz), a curved piece of glass, or something like glass, that will bring closer together or send wider apart the rays of light passing through it. The lens of a telescope makes things look larger. *noun, plural* **lens·es.**

leop·ard (lep′ərd), a fierce animal of Africa and Asia, having a dull-yellowish fur spotted with black. Some leopards are black and may be called panthers. See picture. *noun.*

lev·er (lev′ər *or* lē′vər), bar for raising or moving a weight at one end by pushing down at the other end. It must be supported at any point in between. *noun.*

lin·ger (ling′gər), stay on; go slowly, as if unwilling to leave: *She lingered after the others had left. verb.*

lip-read (lip′rēd′), understand, as by a deaf person, the movements of another's lips when forming words. *verb.*

long·horn (lông′hôrn′), one of a breed of cattle with very long horns, that was seen in the southwestern United States. See picture. *noun.*

loy·al·ty (loi′əl tē), a feeling of being faithful. *noun, plural* **loy·al·ties.**

lul·la·by (lul′ə bī), a soft song to lull a baby to sleep. *noun, plural* **lul·la·bies.**

lum·ber (lum′bər), move along heavily and noisily; roll along with difficulty: *The old stagecoach lumbered down the road. verb.*

M

ma·gi·cian (mə jish′ən), **1** person who can use magic: *The wicked magician cast a spell over the prince.* **2** person who entertains by magic tricks: *The magician pulled three rabbits out of his hat! noun.*

mag·ni·fy (mag′nə fī), cause to look larger than the real size: *A microscope magnifies insects so they can be seen and studied. verb,* **mag·ni·fied, mag·ni·fy·ing.**

man·ag·er (man′ə jər), person who controls: *She is the manager of the store. noun.*

marsh·mal·low (märsh′mal′ō *or* märsh′mel′ō), a soft, white, spongy candy, covered with powdered sugar. *noun.*

ma·ter·i·al (mə tir′ē əl), what a thing is made from or done with: *dress material, building materials, writing materials, the material of which history is made. noun.*

mer·cy (mėr′sē), **1** kindness beyond what can be claimed or expected: *The judge showed mercy to the young man.* **2** something to be thankful for: *It's a mercy you weren't hurt in the accident. noun, plural* **mer·cies.**

mer·ry (mer′ē), full of fun; loving fun; laughing and gay: *a merry laugh. adjective,* **mer·ri·er, mer·ri·est.**

me·squite (me skēt′), a tree or shrub common in the southwestern United States and Mexico. Mesquite often grows in thick clumps. See picture. *noun.*

mi·cro·scope (mī′krə skōp), instrument with a lens or combination of lenses for making small things look larger. Bacteria, blood cells, and other objects too small to see with the naked eye can be seen clearly through a microscope. *noun.*

mi·rac·u·lous (mə rak′yə ləs), **1** going against the known laws of nature: *The miraculous spring water was supposed to make old people young again.* **2** wonderful; marvelous: *miraculous good luck. adjective.*

mo·bile (mō′bēl), decorations hanging from fine wires or threads that move in a slight breeze. See picture. *noun.*

move·ment (müv′mənt), moving: *We run by movements of the legs. noun.*

mu·si·cal (myü′zə kəl), **1** of music: *a musical instrument, a musical composer.* **2** sounding beautiful or pleasing; like music: *a musical voice.*

3 set to music or accompanied by music: *a musical performance.*
4 musical comedy. 1, 2, 3 *adjective,* 4 *noun.*

mys·ter·y (mis′tər ē), **1** a secret; something that is hidden or unknown: *What was in the box was a mystery.* **2** something that is not explained or understood: *the mystery of life on other planets. noun, plural* **mys·ter·ies.**

N

neck·lace (nek′lis), string of jewels, gold, silver, or beads worn around the neck as an ornament. *noun.*

night·in·gale (nīt′n gāl), a small reddish-brown bird of Europe. The nightingale sings sweetly at night as well as in the daytime. *noun.*

nom·i·nate (nom′ə nāt), **1** name as candidate for an office: *He was nominated for President, but he was never elected.* **2** appoint to an office: *In 1933 Roosevelt nominated the first woman cabinet member in United States history. verb,* **nom·i·nat·ed, nom·i·nat·ing.**

non·sense (non′sens), foolish talk or doings: *That tale about the ghost is nonsense. noun.*

nor·mal (nôr′məl), regular; usual: *The normal temperature of the human body is 98.6 degrees. adjective.*

no·ti·fy (nō′tə fī), let know; announce to; inform: *Our teacher notified us that there would be a test on Monday. verb,* **no·ti·fied, no·ti·fy·ing.**

nudge (nuj), **1** push slightly; jog with the elbow to attract attention. **2** a slight push or jog. 1 *verb,* **nudged, nudg·ing;** 2 *noun.*

nurs·er·y (nėr′sər ē), **1** room set apart for the care of babies. **2** a place where small children are cared for during the day: *a day nursery. noun, plural* **nurs·er·ies.**

O

o·cean (ō′shən), **1** the great body of salt water that covers almost ¾ of the earth's surface; the sea. **2** any of its four main divisions—the Atlantic, Pacific, Indian, and Arctic oceans. *noun.*

of·fi·cer (ô′fə sər), person who holds a public, church, or government office: *a health officer, a police officer. noun.*

o·ver·work (ō′vər wėrk′ *for* 1; ō′vər wėrk′ *for* 2), **1** too much or too hard work: *tired from overwork.* **2** work too hard or too long. 1 *noun,* 2 *verb.*

P

pair (per *or* par), **1** set of two; two that go together: *a pair of shoes, a pair of horses.* **2** arrange or be arranged in pairs: *My socks are neatly paired in a drawer.* 1 *noun, plural* **pairs** *or* **pair;** 2 *verb.*

pal·ace (pal′is), **1** a grand house for a king or queen to live in. **2** a very fine house or building. *noun.*

pan·try (pan′trē), a small room in which food, dishes, silver, or table linen is kept. *noun, plural* **pan·tries.**

par·rot (par′ət), bird with a stout, hooked bill and often with bright-colored feathers. Some parrots can imitate sounds and repeat words and sentences. *noun.*

pearl (pėrl), a white or nearly white gem that has a soft shine like satin. Pearls are found inside the shell of a kind of oyster, or in other similar shellfish. See picture. *noun.*

peas·ant (pez′nt), farmer of the working class in Europe. *noun.*

pe·di·a·tri·cian (pē′dē ə trish′ən), doctor who specializes in the care of babies and children. See picture. *noun.*

peer (pir), look closely to see clearly: *He peered at the name on the paper. verb.*

a hat	oi oil	ə stands for:
ā age	ou out	a in about
ä far	u cup	e in taken
e let	u̇ put	i in pencil
ē equal	ü rule	o in lemon
ėr term	ch child	u in circus
i it	ng long	
ī ice	sh she	
o hot	th thin	
ō open	ŦH then	
ô order	zh measure	

pearl—pearl necklace

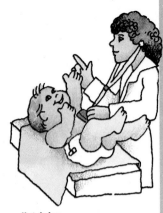

pediatrician

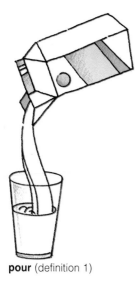

pour (definition 1)

raise (definition 1)

raising the flag

pen·nant (pen′ənt), flag, usually long and narrow, used on ships, in signaling, or as a school banner. In some sports, the best team wins a pennant. *noun.*

per·son·al (pèr′sə nəl), **1** belonging to a person; private: *a personal letter.* **2** done in person: *a personal visit. adjective.*

pi·an·o (pē an′ō), a musical instrument whose tones come from many wires. The wires are sounded by hammers that are worked by striking keys on a keyboard. *noun, plural* **pi·an·os.**

po·em (pō′əm), form of writing in verse; an arrangement of words in lines with a regularly repeated accent and often with rhyme. *noun.*

po·lice (pə lēs′), **1** persons whose duty is keeping order and arresting people who break the law. **2** department of government that keeps order and arrests persons who break the law. *noun.*

po·li·o (pō′lē ō), a disease most often of children that causes fever, paralysis of muscles, and sometimes death. *noun.*

pol·i·tics (pol′ə tiks), science and art of government: *The senator was engaged in politics for many years. noun singular or plural.*

pop·u·lar (pop′yə lər), liked by most people: *a popular song. adjective.*

pos·si·ble (pos′ə bəl), **1** capable of being true or a fact: *It is possible that they are lost.* **2** able to be done or chosen properly: *the only possible action, the only possible candidate. adjective.*

pour (pôr), **1** flow in a steady stream: *I poured the milk from the bottle into the cups.* See picture. **2** a heavy rain; downpour. **1** *verb,* **2** *noun.*

pre·vent (pri vent′), **1** keep from: *Illness prevented him from doing his work.* **2** keep from happening: *Rain prevented the game. verb.*

pre·ven·tion (pri ven′shən), **1** preventing: *the prevention of fire.* **2** something that prevents. *noun.*

pri·vate (prī′vit), personal; not public: *the private life of a king, a private opinion. A diary is private. adjective.*

pro·ces·sion (prə sesh′ən), something that moves forward; persons marching or riding: *a wedding procession. noun.*

prom·ise (prom′is), **1** words said or written, binding a person to do or not to do something: *You can count on her to keep her promise.* **2** give one's word; make a promise: *They promised to stay till we came.* **1** *noun,* **2** *verb,* **prom·ised, prom·is·ing.**

prove (prüv), **1** show that (a thing) is true and right: *Prove your statement.* **2** turn out; be found to be: *The book proved interesting.* **3** try out; test: *prove a new product. verb,* **proved, proved** or **prov·en, prov·ing.**

Q

queen (kwēn), **1** wife of a king. **2** woman who rules a country and its people. *noun.*

R

raise (rāz), **1** lift up; put up: *Children in school raise their hands to answer a question.* See picture. **2** cause to rise: *The cars raised a cloud of dust.* **3** bring up; make grow; help to grow: *She has raised ten children. verb,* **raised, rais·ing.**

rath·er (raᴛн′ər), more willingly: *I would rather go today than tomorrow. adverb.*

re·al·ize (rē′ə līz), **1** understand clearly: *I realize how hard you worked.* **2** make real: *Her uncle's present made it possible for her to realize the dream of going to college. verb,* **re·al·ized, re·al·iz·ing.**

rec·og·nize (rek′əg nīz), know again: *You have grown so much that I scarcely recognized you. verb,* **rec·og·nized, rec·og·niz·ing.**

re·ply (ri plī′), **1** answer by words or action: *He replied with a shout.* **2** answer: *I didn't hear your reply to the question.* **1** *verb,* **re·plied, re·ply·ing; 2** *noun, plural* **re·plies.**

re·trieve (ri trēv′), get again; recover: *retrieve a lost purse. verb,* **re·trieved, re·triev·ing.**

rhyme (rīm), **1** sound alike in the last part: *"Long" and "song" rhyme.* **2** a word or line having the same last sound as another: *"Hey! diddle, diddle" and "The cat and the fiddle" are rhymes.* **1** *verb,* **rhymed, rhym·ing; 2** *noun.*

rick·shaw (rik′shô), a small two-wheeled hooded cart pulled by one or two men, used in Japan and elsewhere. *noun.*

S

sac·ri·fice (sak′rə fīs), **1** giving up one thing for another: *Our teacher does not approve of any sacrifice of studies to sports.* **2** give up: *to sacrifice one's life for another.* **1** *noun,* **2** *verb,* **sac·ri·ficed, sac·ri·fic·ing.**

scarce·ly (skers′lē *or* skars′lē), not quite; barely: *We could scarcely see the ship through the thick fog. adverb.*

scene (sēn), **1** time, place, and events of a play or story: *The scene of the book is laid in Boston.* **2** part of an act of a play: *The king comes to the castle in Act I, Scene 2. noun.*

scheme (skēm), plan: *He has a scheme for catching the robber. noun.*

scold (skōld), blame with angry words: *I scolded them for misbehaving. verb.*

scraw·ny (skrô′nē), thin; skinny: *Turkeys have scrawny necks. adjective,* **scraw·ni·er, scraw·ni·est.**

scroll (skrōl), roll of paper, especially one with writing on it. See picture. *noun.*

ser·ies (sir′ēz), number of things or events happening one after the other: *The cartoon showed a series of pictures. noun, plural* **ser·ies.**

serv·ant (sėr′vənt), person who works in a household. Cooks and nursemaids are servants. *noun.*

serv·ice (sėr′vis), **1** being useful to others: *They gave their services to the hospital.* **2** supply; arrangements for supplying: *Bus service was good. noun.*

shal·low (shal′ō), not deep: *shallow water, a shallow dish. adjective.*

sha·man (shä′mən *or* sham′ən), a medicine man. *noun.*

shoul·der (shōl′dər), part of the body to which the arm is attached. *noun.*

shrug (shrug), raise the shoulders: *He shrugged his shoulders when we asked for directions. verb,* **shrugged, shrug·ging.**

shut·ter (shut′ər), **1** a movable cover for a window: *We closed the shutters as the storm came near.* **2** a movable cover or slide for closing an opening. The device that opens and closes in front of the film in a camera is the shutter. *noun.*

sig·na·ture (sig′nə chər), **1** a person's name written by that person. **2** signs printed at the beginning of a staff to show the pitch, key, and time of a piece of music. *noun.*

skil·let (skil′it), a pan with a handle, used for frying. See picture. *noun.*

slick·er (slik′ər), a waterproof coat. *noun.*

slith·er (sliᴛʜ′ər), to go or walk with a sliding movement: *The snake slithered on the grass. verb,* **slith·ered, slith·er·ing.**

slump (slump), **1** drop heavily; fall suddenly: *slump into a chair.* **2** a great or sudden fall in performance: *Our team is having a slump.* **1** *verb,* **2** *noun.*

a	hat	oi	oil	ə	stands for:
ā	age	ou	out		a in about
ä	far	u	cup		e in taken
e	let	ù	put		i in pencil
ē	equal	ü	rule		o in lemon
ėr	term	ch	child		u in circus
i	it	ng	long		
ī	ice	sh	she		
o	hot	th	thin		
ō	open	ᴛʜ	then		
ô	order	zh	measure		

scroll

skillet

385

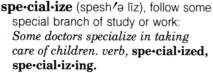

stalk—cat **stalking** a bird

sundial

so·ci·e·ty (sə sī′ə tē), **1** all the people; human beings living together as a group: *Society must work hard for world peace.* **2** fashionable people or their doings: *His parents are leaders of society.* noun, plural **so·ci·e·ties.**

spe·cial·ize (spesh′ə līz), follow some special branch of study or work: *Some doctors specialize in taking care of children.* verb, **spe·cial·ized, spe·cial·iz·ing.**

sprawl (sprôl), lie or sit with the arms and legs spread out: *The people sprawled on the beach in their bathing suits.* verb.

square (skwer or skwar), **1** figure with four equal sides and four right angles (□). **2** space in a city or town bounded by streets on all sides: *This square is full of stores.* noun.

sta·di·um (stā′dē əm), place shaped like an oval or a U, having seats around an open field: *The stadium was filled for the final baseball game.* noun.

stag·ger (stag′ər), sway or rock (from weakness or a heavy load): *I staggered and fell under the heavy load of books.* verb, **stag·gered, stag·ger·ing.**

stalk (stôk), follow without being seen or heard: *The hungry lion stalked a zebra.* See picture. verb, **stalked, stalk·ing.**

stam·pede (stam pēd′), a runaway herd of cattle or horses. noun.

stare (ster or star), **1** look long and directly with the eyes wide open: *The little girl stared at the toys in the window.* **2** a long and direct look with the eyes wide open. **3** be very striking or glaring: *His eyes stared with anger.* 1,3 verb, **stared, star·ing;** 2 noun.

stew (stü or styü), food cooked by slow boiling: *beef stew.* noun.

strum (strum), play by running the fingers lightly across the strings or keys: *strum a guitar.* verb, **strummed, strum·ming.**

strung (strung), stretched the strings across the instrument, such as a violin or a guitar: *She strung her violin before the concert.* verb.

stu·di·o (stü′dē ō or styü′dē ō), **1** workroom of a painter, photographer, or other artist. **2** place where motion pictures are made. noun, plural **stu·di·os.**

suf·fer (suf′ər), have pain, grief, or injury: *He suffers from headaches.* verb.

sug·gest (səg jest′), **1** bring to mind: *The thought of summer suggests swimming, tennis, and hot weather.* **2** put forward; propose: *She suggested we have lunch.* **3** show in an indirect way; hint: *His yawns suggested that he would like to go to bed.* verb.

suit (süt), set of clothes to be worn together. A man's suit consists of a coat, trousers, and sometimes a vest. *The knight wore a suit of armor.* noun.

sun·di·al (sun′dī′əl), instrument for telling the time of day by the way a shadow is cast by the sun. See picture. noun.

T

tel·e·vi·sion (tel′ə vizh′ən), device on which pictures and sounds may be seen and heard. noun.

term (tėrm), a set period of time; length of time that a thing lasts: *The President's term of office is four years.* noun.

ter·rif·ic (tə rif′ik), **1** causing great fear: *A terrific earthquake shook Japan.* **2** very great or severe: *A terrific hot spell ruined many of the crops.* **3** very good; wonderful: *She is a terrific tennis player.* adjective.

thrive (thrīv), turn out well; prosper: *Flowers will not thrive without sunshine.* verb, **throve** or **thrived, thriv·ing.**

ti·pi (tē′pē), a tent used by Native Americans. *noun.*

tis·sue (tish′ü), **1** mass of cells forming part of an animal or plant: *The teacher showed pictures of brain tissues and skin tissues.* **2** a thin, soft paper. *noun.*

to·mor·row (tə môr′ō), **1** the day after today. **2** the near future: *Houses of tomorrow may be heated by the sun. noun.*

trail drive (trāl′ drīv′), the taking of cattle from one place to another: *The cowboys took the cattle on a trail drive. noun.*

trudge (truj), **1** go on foot; walk. **2** a hard or tired walk: *It was a long trudge up the hill.* **1** *verb,* **trudged, trudg·ing; 2** *noun.*

tum·ble·weed (tum′bəl wēd′), plant growing in the western United States that breaks off from its roots and is blown about by the wind. See picture. *noun.*

tun·nel (tun′l), an underground passage: *The railroad passes under the mountain through a tunnel. noun.*

twi·light (twī′līt′), the faint light reflected from the sky before the sun rises and after it sets. *noun.*

ty·rant (tī′rənt), **1** person who uses his power cruelly or unjustly: *A good teacher is never a tyrant.* **2** a cruel or unjust ruler. *noun.*

U

un·snarl (un snärl′), to untangle: *She unsnarled her hair. verb,* **un·snarled, un·snarl·ing.**

V

vet·er·i·nar·i·an (vet′ər ə ner′ē ən), doctor or surgeon who treats animals. See picture. *noun.*

vic·tor·y (vik′tər ē), a win: *The game ended in a victory for our school. noun, plural* **vic·tor·ies.**

vi·o·lin (vī′ə lin′), a musical instrument with four strings played with a bow. *noun.*

W

war (wôr), **1** fighting carried on by armed force between nations or parts of a nation. **2** any fighting or struggle: *Doctors carry on war against disease. noun.*

war·ri·or (wôr′ē ər), a person experienced in fighting battles. *noun.*

whis·tle (hwis′əl), **1** make a clear, shrill sound: *The girl whistled and her dog ran to her quickly.* See picture. **2** sound made by whistling. **3** instrument for making whistling sounds: *The policeman blew his whistle.* **1** *verb,* **whis·tled, whis·tling; 2,3** *noun.*

Y

yes·ter·day (yes′tər dē), **1** the day before today: *Yesterday was cold and rainy.* **2** on the day before today: *It rained yesterday.* **3** the recent past: *We are often amused by the fashions of yesterday.* **1,3** *noun,* **2** *adverb.*

Z

zith·er (zith′ər), a musical instrument having 30 to 40 strings, played with the fingers. *noun.*

a	hat	oi	oil	ə stands for:
ā	age	ou	out	a in about
ä	far	u	cup	e in taken
e	let	ù	put	i in pencil
ē	equal	ü	rule	o in lemon
ėr	term	ch	child	u in circus
i	it	ng	long	
ī	ice	sh	she	
o	hot	th	thin	
ō	open	ŦH	then	
ô	order	zh	measure	

tumbleweed

veterinarian

whistle (definition 1)
girl **whistling**

Page 201: Dramatization of *Juan Bobo and the Queen's Necklace*, A Puerto Rican Folk Tale, Told by Pura Belpré, Copyright © 1962 by Pura Belpré. Adapted by arrangement with Viking Penguin Inc.
Page 234: From *Jump-Rope Rhymes* edited by Roger D. Abrahams. Copyright © 1969 by the American Folklore Society. Reprinted by permission of The University of Texas Press.
Page 277: From the book *Rickshaw to Horror* by Robert Quackenbush. Copyright © 1984 by Robert Quackenbush. Published by Prentice-Hall, Inc., Englewood Cliffs, NJ. Reprinted by permission.
Page 299: *Evan's Corner* by Elizabeth Starr Hill. Copyright © 1967 by Elizabeth Starr Hill. Adapted by permission of Harold Ober Associates Incorporated.
Page 318: *Old Blue* by Sibyl Hancock, text copyright © 1980 by Sibyl Hancock, reprinted by permission of G. P. Putnam's Sons.

Artists
Reading Warm-up: Richard Bernal, 9-23
Section 1: Lydia Halverson, 26, 27, 28, 55; Jean Helmer, 54; Carl Kock, 42, 44, 52
Section 2: Carl Kock, 73, 105; Blanche Sims, 106, 108
Section 3: Bill and Judie Anderson, 177; Robert Baumgartner, 140; Burt Dodsen, 143-151, 153, 155, 157; Elizabeth Miles, 160-163, 165-167, 169, 170, 172, 173, 174; Sandy Rabinowitz, 131-138; Gail Roth, 126-127; Blanche Sims, 128-130, 159; Jack Wallen, 141
Section 4: Andrea Eberbach, 219; Marla Frazee, 178-179; Laurie Jordan, 234-236; Jared D. Lee, 183-198; Karen Loccisano, 181, 218; Dick Martin, 201, 203, 204, 206, 209, 210, 211, 213, 216, 235
Section 5: Shirley Beckes, 240-242, 260; Jackie Geyer, 238-239; Diana Magnuson, 277-279, 281-283, 286, 288-290; Robert Quackenbush, 277-279, 281-283, 286, 288-291; Slug Signorino, 258, 276
Section 6: Shirley Beckes, 260, 352, 365; Jim Cummins, 299, 300, 302, 306, 308, 310, 312, 315; Laura Lydecker, 317; Steve Schindler, 334-347; Jerry Scott, 296-298; John Weeks, 318-321, 323-330
Glossary: George Suyeoka

Freelance Photography
Michael Goss, 49, 51, 53

Picture Credits
Pages 24-25: Norman R. Thompson/TAURUS PHOTOS, INC.; Pages 42, 44-47, 50: Courtesy Pat Sass, Lincoln Park Zoo; Page 48: Susan Reich/The Lincoln Park Zoological Society; Pages 70-71: Joseph A. Di Chello Jr.; Page 72: Marbeth © 1985; Page 74: E. A. McGee/FPG; Page 79: (top right) Marbeth © 1985; Page 79: (bottom right) Shostal Associates; Page 81: © Robert Holmes; Page 82: Roland & Sabrina Michaud/Woodfin Camp & Assoc.; Page 83: © Robert Holmes; Page 84: Field Museum of Natural History; Page 85: Shostal Associates; Page 86: Cameramann Intl., Ltd.; Page 87: Cincinnati Art Museum, Gift of William H. Doane; Page 88: (left) Shostal Associates; Page 88: (top right) From the book MUSICAL INSTRUMENTS THROUGH THE AGES. Collection of Classical Antiquities, Munich; Page 88: (bottom right) Marbeth © 1985; Page 89: Richard Rowan; Page 182: Ewing Galloway; page 220: "Mental Block," a film by Doug S. Chiang © 1984; Pages 221, 222: From ANIMATED FILM, CONCEPTS, METHODS, USES by Dr. Roy Madsen, Copyright © 1969. Reprinted by permission of Dr. Roy Madsen; Page 223: John Marmaras/Woodfin Camp & Assoc.; Page 224: (top) © Walt Disney Productions; page 224: (bottom) © 1937 Walt Disney Productions; Page 225: Jon Wokuluk from "No, No, Pickle"; Page 226: Catherine Hardwicke, Director of "Puppy Does the Gumbo"; Page 227: From "Tuesday" © 1981 by Carl Bressler; Page 228: From "Neighbors" by Norman McLaren, courtesy National Film Board of Canada; Page 229: Camilla Smith/Rainbow; Page 230: (top left and bottom left) Tomas J. Filsinger/Computer Science Graphics Laboratory, UCLA; Page 230: (right) Dan McCoy/Rainbow; Page 232: (left) Catherine Hardwicke, Director of "Puppy Does the Gumbo"; Page 232: (center) From "The Wizard of Speed and Time" by Mike Jittlov; Page 232: (right) © Celia Mercer 1985 "Swimming"; Page 245: (top right and center right) Macmillan Science Co., Inc.,; Page 246: (top left) Mead Johnson Research Center; Page 246: (top right and bottom right) Centers for Disease Control, Atlanta, GA 30333; Page 249: (left) National Livestock and Meat Board; Page 250: (left) ANIMALS ANIMALS/George K. Bryce; Page 250: (right) ANIMALS ANIMALS/Breck P. Kent; Page 262-263: (bottom) © William Curtsinger; Page 263: (top 3 photos) Marty Snyderman; Page 265: Kevin Whitcomb; Page 266: © John G. Shedd Aquarium; Page 267: Howard Hall; Page 268: Ed Robinson/TOM STACK & ASSOCIATES; Page 272: Nicholas Conte/BRUCE COLEMAN INC., New York; Page 273: (top) Kewalo Basin Marine Mammal Laboratory, University of Hawaii; Page 273: (bottom left) David Doubilet; Page 273: (bottom right) © William Curtsinger; Page 274: Marty Snyderman; Page 275: ANIMALS ANIMALS/Jerry Cooke; Pages 294-295: Tom Stack/TOM STACK & ASSOCIATES; Page 366: (top) Carlton C. McAvey.

Cover Artist
John Wallner